MW00812713

UNNATURAL

Niki & Jenny.
Blessings & love.

Rachel M

UNNATURAL

Spiritual Resiliency in Queer Christian Women

Rachel Murr

FOREWORD BY
Jennifer Knapp

RESOURCE *Publications* · Eugene, Oregon

UNNATURAL
Spiritual Resiliency in Queer Christian Women

Copyright © 2014 Rachel Murr. All rights reserved. Except for brief quotations in critical publications or reviews, no part of this book may be reproduced in any manner without prior written permission from the publisher. Write: Permissions. Wipf and Stock Publishers, 199 W. 8th Ave., Suite 3, Eugene, OR 97401.

Resource Publications
An Imprint of Wipf and Stock Publishers
199 W. 8th Ave., Suite 3
Eugene, OR 97401

www.wipfandstock.com

ISBN 13: 978-1-62564-740-5

Manufactured in the U.S.A.   07/07/2014

Scripture quotations labeled NIV are from the Holy Bible, New International Version®. NIV®. Copyright © 1973, 1978, 1984, 2011 by Biblica, Inc.™ Used by permission of Zondervan. All rights reserved worldwide. www.zondervan.com

Scripture quotations labeled NLT are from the *Holy Bible*, New Living Translation, copyright © 1996, 2004, 2007 by Tyndale House Foundation. Used by permission of Tyndale House Publishers, Inc., Carol Stream, Illinois 60188. All rights reserved.

Scripture quotations labeled NRSV are from the New Revised Standard Version of the Bible, copyright © 1989, by the Division of Christian Education of the National Council of the Churches of Christ in the United States of America. Used by permission. All rights reserved.

For the exiles

Contents

Foreword

IF I WERE TO pick the foremost enemy of LGBT spiritual, physical, and psychological health it would be *silence*. The kind of silence that refuses all invitations to speak, to be heard, and welcome empathy. A kind of silence that overpowers the human need for connection and expression. Silence can be the thief of dignity, of respect, of self-knowing and acceptance.

Intrinsically, we somehow understand the difference between the peaceful, noiselessness of sanctuary and the imposter of enforced speechlessness. It is the difference between choosing to be at rest and being tied down against one's will. Both may be equally motionless, but the results are distinctly polarized.

The challenge faced by many who come out inside or near faith community is the near guarantee that in doing so, one is forced to contend with fighting against a religious response which insists on either binding up, changing, and even silencing the gay voice. For many, the "good" Christian is obligated to struggle, twist, and fight for that which is so often taught as "best": heterosexuality. As a result, those who cannot fight or do not wish to fight are summarily disregarded. Their testimonies and experiences shrugged off as moot, without ever acknowledging that their coming out is just as legitimate, necessary, and important a part of the spiritual life as any confession or revelation.

Using the traditional vehicle of Christian testimony, Rachel and the women sharing their stories here in *Unnatural* reveal, what may be for some, a surprising insight into the necessity of restoring religious dignity and sacred space for the LGBT community. It is precisely because we continue to practice personal revelation to our loved ones and neighbors that we begin to understand that the human experience is, in fact, diverse. Diverse in religious practice, approaches to scripture interpretation, and moral conduct, as well as diverse in how we see ourselves through the lens of our sexual orientation and gender.

The interesting time we find ourselves in now is that, as a society, we are coming to understand that homosexuality is no longer a mysterious condition that needs "fixing." People come out every day, so it's worth asking: *Why should I listen to yet another coming out story? Why does it matter?* If sexual orientation and gender identity is being accepted as truly spectral and more fluid than we previously imagined, what more is there to say? An argument could be made that the LGBT community has, at last, broken the silence. There are rainbow flags everywhere. We *are* here, we're queer, but the church at large is still in the process of getting used to us.

Now that the silence has been broken, it is all the more vital that we exercise the opportunity to not only tell our story but to also make the effort to invite these stories to be told as well. Yet by exercising this voice, the cycle of silence is tempted to repeat itself if we do not continue to move forward.

"Loud and proud" (the phenomenon of LGBT people proclaiming and claiming their identity) has been successful to the point that most people in this world have begun to realize that they know and probably love at least one person who is gay. Unfortunately, too many religious communities and leaders have treated this joyous occasion as if it were an epidemic, as if suddenly there has been an unusual outbreak of homosexuality. So much so that many Christians feel it is their duty to reinforce with even louder and sterner voices a proclamation that homosexuality is undeniably *unnatural*.

Thanks to decades' worth of mounting testimony of one brave LGBT person after another, what we are discovering is that the only thing that needs to be changed is how we treat one another, particularly in view of faith and the LGBT people who wish to stay connected with their church families.

Today, religious communities are struggling to keep up with the rising tide of compassion, understanding, and myth busting that has come from the dam having opened its valves. Gay isn't a new, fashionable trend nor is it an epidemic. The reality is that we have been here all along. With renewed strength, support, and a society that is making an invitation to hear our unique stories of experience, LGBT isn't just an identity, it's just life.

What may be even more astonishing is that in living our lives out in the open, we have discovered that we are not without spiritual need. No. Being both gay *and* Christian is not a new trend either. While the stories may have been out of sight of the churches unable to accept their LGBT sons and daughters, we have been growing, praying, and healing spiritual wounds through the very faith practices that insisted there was no place for us. Against all odds, through our living and discovery, we have actually found ourselves in a place to be able to testify to the hope we have found.

It is my hope that you will read this book and discover a portion of your own journey here. Whether you are ready to toss the religious experience aside or are desperately holding to it, there is a little something here that reaches beyond the Christian culture war of gay faith inclusion. Here we have an opportunity to explore how it is religion has been both friend and foe to LGBT people, as well as spend some time examining the purposed and the accidental theologies that have led many Christians down a path of belief that has come to define faith beyond any measure but the human heart.

For anyone, and I mean anyone, gay or straight, that has grown up in, adopted, worked in, or worshipped in Christian community, there is space to recognize that the struggle to understand and own one's faith is always precarious and unique to one's own experience. For everyone that has ever dared tread the path of a spiritual life knows the only certainty is that there will be doubt, questions, and hardships, along with the blessings. As to when, where, and what form any of these experiences will take or how they will play out will be as diverse as our own uniqueness. For those whose sexuality and gender break the norm, it is but one path of discovery, yet oddly, no different than any other journeyman curious and willing to go after one's faith. But you'd have to hear the story to believe it. . . .

Jennifer Knapp

Author Notes

ON PRIVACY

This book is made up of real life stories. In order to protect the privacy of others, names have been changed in the author's story and in the stories of interview participants. Names of churches and colleges have been changed when they have been portrayed in a negative light, unless they are no longer in existence. Some interview participants preferred to be named, including Amy, Jacqueline, Laurie, and Lawrence. The others have been given a pseudonym.

ON QUOTATIONS

Information was gathered through personal interviews. When speaking off the cuff, people often add fillers, repeat themselves, and speak hesitantly in ways that diminish effectiveness in written word. Quotations have been edited in order to make the speaker's point clear and to reduce fillers that do not add to their message.

Example of Original Transcript

"I had no idea honestly what to believe, because my whole life you're taught one thing and then all of a sudden you start feeling a different way. Then you feel like God's abandoned you. But I was seventeen, I always struggled, I had such a hard time during the year with myself with my sexuality. And I'd go up north to camp and get away, go canoeing in the Boundary Waters for like a month—loved it, and that's when I would reconnect with God. I always had such a strong faith afterwards."

Modified Quotation Found in this Book

"I had no idea what to believe, because my whole life you're taught one thing and then all of a sudden you start feeling a different way. Then you feel like God's abandoned you. I was seventeen; I had such a hard time during that year with myself, with my sexuality. I'd go up north to camp and get away, go canoeing in the Boundary Waters for a month. That's when I would reconnect with God. I always had such a strong faith afterwards."

Acknowledgments

So many people have helped me to make this book possible. My first thank you goes to those who were willing to share their stories with me. I was so inspired by your strength, wisdom, faith, and loving-kindness that I could not just keep your stories to myself. Your stories have already made a difference and I'm certain they will continue to do so. Thank you for your honesty and courage. You all have truly changed my life for the better.

I'd like to thank those who saw my writing and my research assignments and encouraged me to continue the work; my social work professors at St. Thomas University and the University of St. Catherine, especially Mari Ann Graham and Katharine Hill, encouraged me to take my research project far beyond the classroom and to take on the ridiculous task of writing a book while still in grad school. You were the first to tell me that I have writing talent. Your encouragement helped me to believe that this was possible.

For your feedback and help in making this book better than I ever could've made in on my own, I'd like to thank Jennifer VanderHeide, and, my writing coach, Elizabeth Jarret Andrew. Honest and helpful feedback is hard to come by, and your thoughts have been immensely helpful. Thank you to my editor, Susan Matheson, for seeing the details that I cannot, for the life of me, see and for providing encouragement and helpful critique. Your commitment to this project is so appreciated.

A heartfelt thank you to all of my friends of my old church, whom I love dearly, especially those who showed me support and advocated for my leadership after I came out. You listened to me and trusted my wisdom, you bravely stood with me, you risked your jobs, you faced criticism, and you suffered loss in your relationships. You kept me in your lives after I left your church and you continue to be my strongest supports. Thank you for showing me grace when I've been angry and resentful. I love you.

Acknowledgments

Mom and Dad, you are tireless advocates and devoted parents. Thank you for all the ways you show me support and encouragement. You always make me laugh. I am sorry that things have not always been easy between us, but I am so thankful for the relationship we have today. I love that I am able to share more of my life with you than ever before and that we understand each another again. You've made me who I am, and I'm finally so happy to be me. I love you both and always have.

1

The Queer Faith Project

I STOOD ALONE IN my freshman dorm room, thumbing through the list of cocurricular activities that were offered on campus. My original attempts at overcoming my shyness through sheer willpower and forced social interaction were not working out very well. Six weeks into the first semester, I was still short on friends and finding myself sulking alone in my dorm room on Friday nights. I knew I had to get involved in something on campus. As I searched through the list of campus groups provided by the university, I thought about where I might best fit. I had distaste for sororities, I'm not remotely musical, and intramural sports required that you sign up with an entire team already in place. After some deliberation, I narrowed my choices to two options: a campus Christian organization or the gay and lesbian group. I knew it could not be both.

For the next fifteen years I held onto that same belief that I could not be both gay and Christian. At first, this belief came from a fear of being judged or rejected by the Christians rather than a moral objection to being gay. I was well aware of certain Christians' beliefs that it was wrong to be gay, but I wasn't persuaded. I hesitated to visit the gay and lesbian group because I had a sense that if I went once, I'd be labeled for life, or that there would be no turning back. I hadn't yet fully come out to myself, and I wasn't sure that Fargo, North Dakota, would be the best place to do so. Attending the Christian group would definitely be an easier choice. Besides, I figured, they *have* to be nice.

Before I came to a decision, a neighbor invited me to the Christian group. (As it turns out, the Christians were better recruiters.) After attending their weekly meeting, I quickly made friends and found myself in the midst of a supportive, fun, and loving community. The community of believers was healing for me, chipping away at my own feelings of isolation and difference. I began to experience a personal and loving God who cared about me. Staff members of the Christian group saw leadership potential in me and encouraged me to take on new challenges: leading small groups, sharing my testimony, and reaching out to others. God and the Christian community changed my life in wonderful ways.

After my newfound spiritual experiences and the decision to follow Jesus, I slowly adopted the teachings of the campus Christian organization and allowed these teachings to define how to interpret the Bible, what God is like, and how I should live out my faith. During this time I thought that Christianity was a very hard truth. I thought it was a tough pill to swallow, that you had to believe things that don't make a lot of sense—like Jesus is the only way, people go to hell for not believing the right thing, and, of course, that being gay is wrong. I thought that faith was hard and that following Jesus meant being countercultural, even offensive to those outside the faith.

My views have changed a lot since then, but I remain a Christian. I still find meaning in community, worship, solitary prayer, and Scripture. I still seek to follow the way of Jesus and look to the power of the Holy Spirit to live a life of faith. I've completely abandoned the belief that same-sex relationships are inherently sinful. After many years of wrestling with the question of what it means to be lesbian and Christian, eventually I came to believe that loving another woman could be okay with God—that it might even be how God created me.

This change in beliefs took some time. Like most major theological shifts, it took place after significant discomfort with the way I'd been living. My belief that God's laws are for our benefit did not line up with my experience of following what I thought to be God's law about same-gender relationships. I was miserable. In seeking health, I began to question what I'd been taught about homosexuality. I wondered if God had good news for gay people.

During my process of adopting an affirming faith, I needed to hear from other queer (a catch-all term I use for lesbian, gay, bisexual, transgender, or otherwise nonheterosexual) women who've held onto their faith. I needed to know that I did not have to choose between gay or Christian but that it was possible to be both.

TIMES ARE CHANGING

Many others have shifted their views about homosexuality in the past decades as our culture has become more accepting of queer people. The church, of course, has been slower to change. "The gay issue" is the most fiercely debated topic in the Christian church in America as congregations and denominations continue to split over questions of membership, leadership, and ordination of LGBTQ (lesbian, gay, bisexual, transgender, and queer) people. Somehow, the behavior of about five percent of the population has become the most important issue of the church. Clearly something more is at stake. In her memoir, Sara Miles, author and founder of The Food Pantry at St. Gregory of Nyssa Episcopal Church, explains the dynamics well: "It wasn't just about gayness, of course, but a more fundamental conflict between believers who craved certainty and those who embraced ambiguity; those who insisted Scripture was inerrant and unchanging, given once and for all time, and those who believed that the Bible was only part of God's continuing revelation. The struggle was also about how to define a Christian: as one who sought to keep the religion 'pure' or one who welcomed outcasts."[1] She explains that those who want to hold on to tradition and preserve the purity of their movement must exclude all threats. Queer people have come to represent the threat of what conservatives fear most about losing their firmly held belief in the inerrancy of Scripture and certainty about their interpretation of the text. As a result of this fear and the actions stemming from it, religious groups have come to represent hatred and bigotry to many in the LGBTQ community and their allies. This leaves queer people of faith with some major challenges in finding safe places to bring their whole selves into community.

These polarizing dynamics are changing as affirming faith communities have played a huge role in combating religious messages of condemnation. In my home state of Minnesota, faith communities and affirming clergy rallied to defeat the Minnesota Marriage Amendment (a constitutional amendment that was on the ballot in 2012 to ban same-sex marriage) and to advocate for legislation in favor of same-sex marriages. People of faith organized marches, summits, and other public statements showing

1. Miles, *Take This Bread*, 88.

their support for same-sex marriages. No longer can Christians claim that there is one clear and authoritative position of the Christian church. It is truly divided.

As my own church wrestled with these issues a few years ago, I felt the tension. I wondered if staying in my church was good for me. I wondered how others had dealt with the conflict that they may have felt between their faith and sexuality. Did they stay in nonaffirming churches? Did they try to advocate for change? Did they give up on organized religion? I needed to talk to others.

The opportunity to search for other queer believers came about when I was completing my master of social work. Through a year-long research project, I studied the experiences of lesbian and bisexual Christian women from nonaffirming Christian communities to explore how and why they held onto faith. I interviewed eight women, asking about early church culture, messages they heard about LGBTQ people, and their reasons for coming out and reasons for holding onto their faith. I ended each interview by asking participants if their view of God had changed.[2] Their stories were rich. They shared openly of their pain and their joy, their doubts and their convictions. After finishing the project, I didn't want it to be over. I had discovered something beautiful in the lives of these women. They stirred up in me the ridiculous notion to tell my own story, too.

This book is a collection of stories—testimonies about the work of God in the lives of people the church has rejected. In my church tradition, personal testimonies are commonly shared during a Sunday service. Members stand up and tell the community how God has changed their lives in big ways or small. Their stories provide hope to others and reasons for giving thanks to God together. These stories connect people to each other through common life experiences and hardships. On any given Sunday, most of us are far more likely to remember the testimony of a fellow member than the sermon.

There is also something powerful about telling our own stories. Sharing a personal struggle and how God has worked in it is a chance to express our authentic selves, to bring hope to others, and to say, "Look what God has done!" The way we construct our own life stories impacts our sense of self and of the world around us. In mental health professions, there is a specific therapeutic approach, called narrative therapy, which helps clients reconstruct their life stories with new meaning. Narrative therapists

2. Murr, "I Became Proud," 349–72.

seek to point out the larger societal picture, or "meta-narrative," of their clients' lives. They highlight oppressive systems or unjust cultural norms and look for a "counter story," one that highlights the client's strengths. The meta-narrative for queer women may include messages that they are sinful, gross, unspiritual, unhealthy, man haters, and/or a threat to "family values." Acknowledging the reality of this cultural meta-narrative can help individuals see how they have been impacted by harmful messages and how they have resisted them. Any resistance to these messages indicates how individuals have courageously fought against strong, oppressive cultural forces. Through narrative therapy, clients begin reframing life events into a story that can be told for a purpose. This storytelling may be a powerful tool in both seeing a "counter story" of strength in one's own life, and in making meaning out of painful circumstances.

It is my hope that listening closely to the pain and hope and faith in these stories will reveal the work of the Holy Spirit and testify to God's hand in their lives. Just as Peter saw the work of the Spirit among the gentiles before welcoming them into the community of believers,[3] the church needs to see the spirit of God at work among queer people. As Peter preached to his community, "If God gave them the same gift he gave us who believed in the Lord Jesus Christ, who was I to think that I could stand in God's way?"[4]

THE RESEARCH

When it came time to start recruiting people for my research project, I searched for participants through word-of-mouth in the Minneapolis/St. Paul metro area. The Twin Cities are widely considered to be a very safe and supportive place to be both queer and Christian. Minneapolis has a thriving gay community and was named *The Advocate*'s "gayest city" of 2011. Between the liberal politics, the strong arts community, and the deep religious roots, Minnesota has been both progressive and religious. Despite these factors, my interview participants still faced significant challenges finding welcoming communities.

My original project included eight women who identified as lesbian or bisexual and described their current faith as meaningful and affirming. After the research project was complete, I was free to loosen the requirements for participation. At that time, I interviewed two more women and

3. Acts 10:44–11:18.

4. Acts 11:17 (NIV).

one female-to-male transgender man. All participants have identified as Christian for most of their lives; most retained this label, but some did not. While all participants came from "nonaffirming" Christian environments, this term included a wide range of church cultures. Some had church leaders mocking gay people and preaching condemnation from the pulpit, some had an unspoken but clear understanding that it was not okay to be gay, and some had very welcoming communities under the umbrella of a larger denomination that limited their ability to openly acknowledge same-gender unions. All participants had some conflict with their own churches or the greater Christian church, and all report a current meaningful spiritual life.

I started the interviews with a set of eleven predetermined questions, including: "What was the Christian culture you grew up in like?," "What was it like to know you were lesbian or bisexual in your church environment?," "What made you want to hold on to or return to spiritual practice?," and "What is your faith like now?" We generally meandered away from my script as we discussed each person's complex life story, and as participants shared generously of their pain and their faith. I've changed the names of all participants except Amy, Jacqueline, Gretchen, Laurie, and Lawrence, who all requested that I use their real names. A brief description of each participant is provided below for ease of reference and keeping track of various stories.

Most of the interviews took place in local coffee shops of Minneapolis. I came with my digital recorder, a consent form, and a pad of paper for jotting down notes. My participants were all urban Minnesotans, living in or near St. Paul or Minneapolis. They were vastly different in personality, culture, and history. Some grew up in Minnesota, while others had lived in California, Arizona, New York, and Texas. Their ages ranged from early twenties to early fifties. Their church backgrounds were quite diverse, including predominantly black Baptist, white Lutheran, Puerto Rican Pentecostal, evangelical (English and Spanish speaking), and charismatic, as well as Catholic churches that were predominantly white, Hispanic, or racially diverse. The church cultures of the participants varied from silence about homosexuality to open hostility towards queer people. Some participants found affirming congregations later in life in the United Church of Christ, the Metropolitan Community Church, the Evangelical Lutheran Church of America, or Congregational churches. Some decided against organized religion, and some even stayed in nonaffirming churches, hoping to take part in bringing about change.

Despite their very different backgrounds, my participants' current faith practices were not dissimilar. Each of them experienced spiritual transformation as they worked at maintaining (or restoring) a life of faith. I found each person's story deeply moving. They talked about their lives in a way that was candid, inspiring, and full of beauty. They showed strength, resiliency, hope, and a commitment to creating a better world.

AMY

Amy and I met for our interview in a coffee shop in Minneapolis. She was referred to me by her mother, Jacqueline, whom I interviewed later. Amy is in her mid-twenties, barely five foot two, and fairly butch. She wore a buzz cut and dressed in all black. She identified herself as half Puerto Rican and half Jewish but was more heavily influenced by her Puerto Rican heritage, learning Spanish before she learned English and attending Catholic mass in her family of origin and in foster homes. She now attends a predominantly black Baptist church and considers herself conservative and affirming. She told her rather devastating story with an easy-going and slightly cynical sense of humor and we laughed throughout the entire interview. Her story is one of resilience and hope despite rather tragic beginnings.

ANITA

I met Anita through my former Vineyard church. She spoke very positively about her church experiences, both in childhood and as an adult, despite feeling she had to hide a significant relationship for three years. She is Mexican American, and her parents switched from a Catholic church to an evangelical one when she was very young. She doesn't like the labels of lesbian or bisexual, preferring to not be so easily categorized. Her story speaks to the pain involved in hiding oneself from family and friends and her trust in a God who accepts us all.

ERICKA

Ericka was referred to me by another participant, Hannah, because of her unique story. Before meeting her I was told that she was kicked out of her house when she came out as lesbian, resulting in estrangement from her parents for about a year. Just as her mother was coming to accept her, ironically, Ericka started dating an old male friend and got pregnant unexpectedly. Now, they are married and raising their child together. Ericka is Caucasian, nearly thirty, and she grew up in a very strict and frightening religious environment. She still feels the impact of the harsh criticism and messages of judgment she felt in her home and church.

GRETCHEN

Gretchen is the only participant who didn't grow up in the church. She is in her mid-forties and works in the corporate office of a major retail outlet. We met because of her involvement in PFLAG (Parents, Friends and Families of Lesbians and Gays), where she serves on the board of directors. She took up an interest in spiritual things just as she was coming out to herself as a teenager. She drew interesting parallels between serving in the military and taking part in the Christian church, two institutions that did not allow her to serve as an openly gay person but that she believed in nonetheless. Now, she and her wife are very involved in their Lutheran church, which is fully supportive of them.

HANNAH

Hannah and her husband were attending my former church at the time of the interview. She identifies as bisexual, but feels she needs to keep this part of herself hidden from her church friends. She fears the repercussions that would take place if she were more open; for example, she wonders how people would treat her daughter or if she would be denied leadership if she came out. She is in her mid-twenties, average height, with light brown hair. She grew up Catholic and was very involved in LGBTQ advocacy in college. As a suburban mother, she found herself surrounded by conservative Christians who, she felt, would not approve of her if she were more honest.

JACQUELINE

Jacqueline is a writer and advocate for LGBTQ people. She grew up in a Catholic church in the 1960s that was very involved in social justice issues like equal housing and other civil rights. Her experiences of action-oriented faith were formative for her, leading to a lifelong interest in taking up the cause of the underrepresented. Jacqueline is tall with short blonde hair and identifies as bisexual. She sought out a spiritual blessing when her partner transitioned from female to male and was deeply disappointed to discover that they would not be able to get married in her beloved church. We met for the interview in her Minneapolis home where she, Amy (whom she adopted at age nineteen), and her partner were living.

KIMBERLY

I met Kimberly after she starting dating a friend of mine. She is a twenty-something African American woman with long braided hair. She lived in a shelter for homeless teens for several years after getting kicked out of her mother's house because of conflicts about her sexual orientation. She knew she was lesbian at a young age and also knew that her mother would not respond well to this news. Kimberly wishes more queer people could see that you can be gay and Christian "and not hate yourself."

LAURIE

Laurie is a well-known spiritual leader in the local LGBTQ community. She is a minister in the United Church of Christ and lives with her partner in the suburbs. She is in her mid-forties with short, sandy blonde hair. Laurie spent years trying to change her orientation and saw a counselor for the purpose of trying to stop being attracted to women. Eventually she found these efforts to be fruitless and came out at her church. She was careful not to come out before graduating from a conservative Bible college since she had the valid concern that she would be kicked out with just one semester left to graduate. Thankfully, she got her degree and moved on to a progressive theological seminary.

MAUREEN

Maureen is a young attorney who grew up in California. In her Catholic church and family, homosexuality was not talked about, and her family acted as if "it didn't exist almost." Her mother expressed some protest when she came out, but her biggest conflict was with "brutal" Minnesota evangelicals or, in her case, the in-laws. After years of conflict, Maureen and her wife have seen significant growth in their relationships with her wife's family. Still, the conflict changed Maureen, making her a bit gun-shy about having any religious conversations or even saying something as innocuous as "bless you" after a sneeze.

RENAE

I met Renae through some mutual friends. She grew up in a variety of churches, but they all held negative views about homosexuality. She is mixed race with curly, long black hair. Her father, who was African American, died when she was young, leaving her and her brother with just their mom. Renae described her mother as "a tiny little thing" who can "verbally intimidate" through arguments and references to Scripture. She spoke at length about their relationship, their estrangement, and little ways their relationship has improved in recent years. Her story is one of finding health and personal integrity by coming out and surrounding herself with supportive others.

LAWRENCE

Lawrence's story is saved for the end of this book because his story, as a transgender man who transitioned from Lateasha to Lawrence at age twenty-eight, is different than the others. Using his story to draw conclusions about queer women does not make sense because he never felt like a woman. Still, his story is important because he has experienced life in both genders and tells of a profoundly beautiful transformation of his body and spirit. Transgender people typically face more discrimination, violence, and mistreatment than gay and lesbian people, putting them at high risk for depression and suicide. Lawrence's story is important because it offers hope to others and tells of the joy he found after knowing utter misery.

KEPT OUT OF A GOOD THING

I started this project with the deeply held belief that faith communities can provide rich and lasting benefits to their members. I'd experienced these benefits already. My connection to faith communities had challenged me to love the outcasts, to be generous with others, and to find healing for my own wounds. The church had shaped my values and my very identity. Coming out, and the conflict that ensued, made me wonder if church was still good for me. I'd taken in many beliefs about homosexuality that I was beginning to see as harmful. The longer I stayed at my church after coming out, the more painful it was to be there. I wondered if the church was causing more harm than good for me and for other LGBTQ people.

As I researched these questions in psychology and social work journals, there was no doubt about the potential benefits of developing an individual spiritual life. Spirituality has been linked to resiliency among many different people groups, including runaway homeless youth,[5] people recovering from traumatic experiences,[6] and people in poverty.[7] Spiritual beliefs were found to lessen the psychological impact of these hardships and promote positive beliefs about self and God.

An interesting study on trauma and spirituality found that many people who were healing from traumatic events struggled with "existential issues related to the meaning of suffering, the nature of good and evil, [and] their own religious beliefs."[8] Trauma disrupts a person's sense of safety and often raises spiritual questions. Spirituality may support the recovery process by:

- giving definition to who we are
- providing a structure for understanding the world and events that occur
- providing a mechanism to transcend events of this life
- giving a frame of reference for understanding good and evil
- providing a mechanism for forgiveness.[9]

In this study, traits associated with resiliency were linked to traits found in religious and spiritual practice. These overlapping traits include insight, independence, establishing relationships, initiative, creativity, humor, and morality. Spirituality may also aid in resiliency through a belief

---

5. Williams, "Spirituality and Religion," 47–66.
6. Farley, "Making the Connection," 1–15.
7. Bradshaw and Ellison, "Financial Hardship," 106–204.
8. Farley, "Making the Connection," 1–15.
9. Greene, *Resiliency*, summarized by Farley, "Making the Connection," 4.

in divine intervention, use of prayer, and finding purpose in painful life experiences.[10]

In addition to spirituality, organized religion has also been shown to provide substantial benefits to those who take part. Around the world, those who are involved in faith communities report better health, more energy, and better relationships than those who are not religiously involved.[11]

Given the widespread messages of condemnation that come from the mouths of Christians, I wondered if queer people could still benefit from staying connected to the Christian church or if the vocal minority had ruined church for us. As I researched these questions, the results were mixed. One study found that leaving a religious environment led to improved self-esteem for lesbian, gay, and bisexual young adults.[12] Another found that religious involvement in young people carried health benefits for gay and bisexual males age 14 to 21, but lesbian and bisexual females of the same age group experienced no protective benefits from their religious involvement.[13]

I was struck by the absence of research about queer women and their involvement in faith communities. For every study I found exploring generic spirituality in queer women, there were four studies specific to gay Christian men. Others had explored how gay Catholic men, gay black men, and gay black men with AIDS reconcile conflicting religious and sexual identities. The same studies didn't exist for women. Was this just the typical discrepancy in research that favors the male experience? Or, are there other factors that led to a lack of research? I suspect the latter, as lesbian women are more likely to leave faith communities than gay men, straight men, or straight women.[14] My own experience echoed the research. When I visited a local gay church, the ratio of men to women seemed to be at least five to one. This was a problem for me. Even the gay church wasn't attracting gay women! What was getting in the way?

I haven't discovered a clear answer for why queer women have left faith communities at a higher rate than other groups. The most common reason I hear is that the patriarchy and anti-gay views within the church combine to make a double-whammy that keeps most queer women away.

10. Williams, "Spirituality and Religion," 47–66.

11. Deaton, "Aging, Religion and Health," 22–26

12. Ison et al., "A Nietzschean Perspective," 136–53.

13. Rosario et al., "Religion and Health," 117–40.

14. Sherkat, "Sexuality and Religious Commitment," 313–28.

I still believe that following Jesus in community should allow us to experience the "abundant life" of the gospel message. It saddens me that current cultural dynamics make it difficult to reap these benefits.

A common question asked of LGBTQ Christians has been, "Why do you stay involved in a religion that rejects and condemns you?" In my interviews, it was clear that involvement was not about self-loathing, self-discipline, or a sense of obligation. Participants had genuinely benefitted from their faith communities. Church was often a place where they met loving people, had fun, found support, and connected to a greater purpose. Many spoke very lovingly of current and former church communities. Positive early experiences and a sense of "missing something" were often what drew people back to church later in life.

Everyone I interviewed experienced some positive aspects of faith community. They found supportive relationships as well as a sense of purpose, belonging, and connection to God. Their love of their churches made the negative experiences all the more painful. All participants were exposed to harmful messages that went beyond a conservative interpretation of biblical texts and crossed into claims that gay people are inherently damaged, shameful, and threatening. Few can escape these messages because they are so prevalent, permeating faith communities, schools, political advertisements, and other media.

STRUCTURE OF THIS BOOK

This book includes personal memoir, stories from other queer women, and information from research I gathered. These various pieces are organized to loosely follow our narratives, starting with the *messages* we received as children about what it means to be lesbian or bisexual, then moving on to the *impact* these messages had (and have) on us, including mental health issues, family rejection, and loss of beloved communities. Next, I look at how these women were able to *integrate* their spiritual lives and sexual orientation, developing an affirming personal faith. Finally, I explore the ways that participants found health and wholeness after coming out to self and others.

There are eleven different stories, plus my own, so to help the reader keep track of the many different people, I've kept each participant's life story largely within a single chapter. One woman's story may be in the chapter on "Impact," but her story may also speak to integration, negative messages, and finding an abundant life. In my research writing[15] it was important to highlight themes that were present among multiple interview stories. Individual quotes about "messages" or "integration" were organized under those categories. Here, it is more important that the participants' stories shine through, highlighting their personalities, resilience, struggles, and growth.

15. Murr, "I Became Proud," 349–72.

2

Messages: Home and Church

As I was growing up, my family was very involved in our local Catholic church and we went to mass every Sunday. We joked that my mom was "the Church Lady"—Dana Carvey's Saturday Night Live character. My mom stayed busy running the Wednesday night kids' classes and organizing volunteers. She didn't let us off the hook either; we were expected to serve as a family, greeting people at the door on Sunday mornings, taking up the collection, or setting out doughnuts after mass. I found mass to be rather boring and used the time to daydream. By the end of the service, I had no idea what the priest had just said. Our church was fairly progressive by Catholic standards. We had no kneelers or altar boys. Families took turns being ushers, collecting the offerings, and greeting people at the front door with name tags. There wasn't a strong message about conservative moral teaching, nor was there a strong liberal social justice message. The mission was community, and that's what we gained. While my mom found great meaning in the traditions and rituals of the church, the rest of us were along for the ride.

I perceived my childhood to be very normal. I knew I was lucky to have a loving family in a quiet and safe suburban neighborhood. On summer days I biked around the neighborhood, snooped around construction sites, and played tennis barefoot in the driveway with my brother. My family was well respected at church and at school, and all four of us kids got good grades and stayed out of trouble.

Like so many other queer people, I had a sense of being different at an early age. This difference was in part about shyness and in part about queerness—feeling both drawn to and different from the other girls. I worried that I would be discovered for being different, or strange, and wondered what was wrong with me. The word "gay" was still something foreign to me, a dirty word, something that didn't describe anyone I knew. Still, I liked being a tomboy and was proud of how I was usually the first girl picked for dodge ball.

In tenth grade I began to wonder if I might be a lesbian. My disinterest in the boys was growing apparent. And, I was drawn to other girls. I think most of my friends would have supported me coming out, but I still chose to keep quiet. No one at my school was out, and I was unprepared to stand alone. I was fairly certain that my parents would not approve if I told them I was gay. My mom's religious views and my dad's love for conservative talk radio made me think that neither one would be very happy about the news. One memory stands out in my mind of being at church on a Sunday when I was in high school. I was in the midst of deciding where I wanted to go to college. When my dad joked with another church member, saying, "Rachel can't play for the U of M volleyball team because she's not a lesbian," I was amused (as I usually am by my dad's antics). I smiled and thought to myself, "Are you sure about that?" His joke wasn't mean or condemning, just rooted in stereotypes about women in sports and the assumption that gay people are not like "us"—that he would surely know if I were lesbian or not.

As I left for college, I had big dreams of breaking out of my shell and leaving behind the perception that I was shy. I was going where nobody knew me, where I was free to form a new identity. I determined to do everything I could to be social and meet new people. Sadly, change took more than just willpower. I soon admitted that I was just as shy as ever, and I still hadn't found a group of friends to call my own.

My roommate was involved in a Christian group on campus, and she was immediately surrounded by new friends despite her lack of social skills. They all seemed a bit strange to me. They were a little too excited about everyday occurrences, like finding a parking spot or getting an extra bag of chips in a vending machine error. They bowed their heads to pray before eating at the crowded dining center and reacted with shock when I jokingly said such inappropriate things as, "Screw you."

Eventually, some people I'd met down the hall invited me to a meeting of a different Christian group. Here, I met people that seemed interesting, fun, and kind. Still, the Christian culture of this group was strange to me. About a month after attending my first meeting I was invited to go on an overnight retreat at a local hotel. They called it "Evangelism Training." I didn't know what that meant, but I decided to go anyway. During this retreat, I heard a clear explanation of their gospel message. It made sense to me, but I had a lot of questions. Their convictions seemed arrogant to me. How can they say that Jesus is the only way? How can they believe that people go to hell for not being a Christian? Why are they all Republicans?

Later that day, I tagged along with some friends as they started a spiritual conversation with a woman I knew from my dorm. We all sat down on her dorm room floor as we talked. She was surprisingly honest with them and started to cry as she shared that she knew her life was empty and meaningless. She told my friends that she didn't want to pray with them and didn't want to join their group, but she thanked them for talking to her. I snuck off to the bathroom and cried.

I was baffled. I knew this woman; she seemed to have it all. She was attractive, intelligent, outgoing, and genuinely kind. She had everything that I'd been striving for, and she said it was empty. I locked myself in a stall of the bathroom and prayed, "God, I need you. Not as I've been trying to make you, but as you are." That moment I opened my life to Jesus, and I let go of my questions. I began to let this group shape my view of God and humanity—in good ways and bad.

By the time most girls are aware of their own same-sex attraction, they've already been inundated with negative messages about what it means to be lesbian or bisexual. In this chapter we will look at messages that participants in my study heard at home and at church and how those messages were received. In the next two chapters, we'll look at messages from ex-gay ministries and messages from the media, politics, and wider communities.

The women I interviewed placed their first awareness of same-gender attractions anywhere from age four to into their twenties and early thirties. They also had varying interpretations of what that meant based on their family and Christian culture. Most reported experiences of being told that gay people were especially sinful. They often picked up on their community's fear, silence, or anger at a young age. Their experiences varied in severity and some internalized these messages more than others, but all were very familiar with certain Christians' judgment of them.

Perhaps the only institution more influential than the church in instilling messages of either acceptance or condemnation is the family. Well before young people consider coming out to their parents, they have likely picked up on their parents' perceptions of queer people. I knew that my mom's lesbian sister was not someone we talked about and that my dad was a conservative talk show junkie. Between the Pope and Rush Limbaugh, my parents' spiritual and political leaders were not in my favor.

SILENCE

The messages parents pass along to their children may be overt or subtle, but they will communicate their thoughts in one way or another. My parents almost never said anything negative about gay people, but their silence communicated enough for me to think that they wouldn't be thrilled to hear I was lesbian. Several women talked about how silence in their families communicated a great deal about what was acceptable and what wasn't. They learned to hide relationships or hide their feelings in order to avoid difficult topics. As I gathered the stories of other women, I found that many of them came from family backgrounds similar to my own, where no one talked about "that one aunt" (or uncle), and there was an unspoken judgment on them. These environments seem to be far less damaging than homes where anti-gay messages were loud and clear, but the message of silence was still harmful. Gretchen was the only one of my participants who didn't grow up going to church. She didn't join a church until after she completed her military service. Still, she experienced silencing about homosexuality in her family that has continued for decades. She said, "No one in my family ever talks about homosexuality; it was always this thing that you hear out in society, but parents kind of ignore. It's other people. . . . What I didn't know at the time is that one of my aunts was also a lesbian; to this day [she] has completely segregated herself from the family. . . . She's been with her partner for over twenty years, and I've only met her partner once. It's all this unspoken stuff that's really ugly and really damaging." Gretchen has a wife, and still her aunt is unable to be open with Gretchen about the nature of her own twenty-year partnership.

Interestingly, two other women in my study, Maureen and Anita, both described family dynamics of silence, and both carried on the tradition themselves by keeping a relationship hidden from their families for years. Both came out to their families after the relationships ended and they were in need of support, only to find that their well-kept secret was not much of a secret at all. It was something "everybody knows but nobody talks about."

ANITA: "THE ELEPHANT IN THE ROOM"

I met Anita through friends at my former church. After seeing each other at services for a few months, she approached me and said, "This might sound kinda weird, but I think God wants me to invite you to coffee." I figured I better agree. We went for coffee, which opened the door for us to talk about faith and sexuality when neither of us had acknowledged our orientation to the other before. We spoke at length about challenges we faced in being queer and Christian. Anita is Mexican American, in her early thirties. She has an athletic build and long brown hair. She stays active, playing rugby and softball in the summer and snowboarding in the winter. She is laid back and confident, with an easy-going sense of humor.

Later, during the year of my research, Anita moved out of state, so our interview was conducted over the phone. In the interview, I learned about her evangelical background and her reasons for staying faithful to Christianity. Her experiences within evangelical churches were surprisingly positive. She described her early family life: "As far as I can remember back, we were attending some big church. I remember being around four years old when my parents converted from Catholicism to [nondenominational] Christianity. . . . My dad was an elder in the church, and my mom was on the worship team. As we got a little bit older, we ended up going to the Spanish Ministry inside the church." She believed that her parents' involvement in this church changed them for the better and shaped her family in very positive ways. "Growing up and seeing my parents' faith be developed, it also developed mine; watching them be generous with their money, generous with who they were as people. My mom and dad ended up adopting four more kids. There was originally just two of us and they adopted four more later on in life. They were very generous people, very loving and caring people. Being a part of church [and] having a relationship with God molded them, and it molded me as well." Anita seemed certain that being part of a church community is what made her family more loving, caring, and generous.

Anita did not speak about an early awareness of being drawn to other girls. "I really didn't start feeling anything towards [members of the] same-sex until around twenty-four. I was married, and [my husband and I] were separated at the time, and my best friend came into the picture. I knew she was gay and it wasn't until then [that I felt a same-sex attraction]. I've never had a gay friend before. My older brother came out right around the same time. And then a couple [of] cousins here and there or a couple [of] coworkers. But I'd never had really close relationships to know what their lifestyle was like."

Messages she'd learned about homosexuality had an impact in how she reacted to these feelings. "Growing up in the church, we were always taught that homosexuality was a sin. And not only was it a sin, it was a sexual sin. I didn't know what to do about my feelings towards my girlfriend. . . . I constantly questioned myself. I wasn't out to anybody and neither was she, so we hid our relationship for three years. It was quite difficult to carry on, especially around church friends."

Anita described this time as "very, very, difficult," and she clearly suffered in the midst of it. "It didn't validate my relationship if I couldn't share my joy; I couldn't share my ups and downs with people that I loved and I cared about, that loved me just as much. I felt like it wasn't real because I had to hide everything. We finally broke up; she didn't think that I wanted to be in a homosexual relationship, so she ended things."

Despite the love and acceptance she felt in her family, she still decided to hide this relationship from them. She explained the dynamics involved in the pressure she felt to stay silent. "I think my ethnicity has something to do with it—not only being a Christian but being Mexican as well, I think that it's one of those unspoken things. It's known but never talked about, like the giant elephant in the room. Everybody knows it's there, but we don't speak of it."

The dynamic she describes is common to many minority cultures where the social connections are strong and members rarely sever ties. Family units and faith communities may choose to ignore the obvious in order to avoid conflict and maintain relationships within a tightly knit community.

Anita came out to her family after the relationship had already ended. First, she started talking to people at our church. "Just after that breakup I moved to Minnesota. About a year into me living in Minnesota, I was attending the Vineyard church and we went through a Bible series [*They Like Jesus but Not the Church*[1]]. It touched on three different or four different main keys. . . . The first part was dealing with homosexuality—where it fits

1. Kimball, *They Like Jesus*.

in the church and things like that." She said, "I had a real gut feeling that my parents needed to know." She wondered if they knew already, but she wanted to be able to say aloud the truth of her relationship. "After going through that series I remember making a phone call to my mom and telling her about my relationship, and in the next few days calling brothers and sisters in explaining myself as well to them."

When Anita broke the silence and told her family she'd been dating a woman, her father and siblings showed her immediate support. Even though her father had been critical of gay people in the past, he expressed love and acceptance of his daughter. Her mom had more trouble and told Anita that she already knew about the relationship. "She said she knew and that she [had been] pray[ing] every day that we would break up—that God would break us up, that it wasn't right."

Over time, her mom showed progress in being more supportive, keeping any disapproval she may have felt to herself. "She's come along quite a bit. I mean, she's at least a little bit more accepting of it. You can tell she's not totally comfortable with it but she will make an effort to know what's going on in my life and who I might be dating."

Anita credits the strong relationship she has with her family as the most influential factor in her parents' changing perceptions about gay people. "We grew up believing that homosexuality was immoral and a sin. Until someone you know, someone you love very much is put in that position . . . I don't think their opinions would've changed. But since it was their daughter, they started to open up their eyes a little bit more and see me for who I really am, and that was just a child of God. No matter if I was gay or straight or bisexual or whatever I wanted to be, that they were still going to love me just the same."

Her family's love and acceptance had a huge impact on her and her own ability to find an integrated faith. She said, "As long as my mom and dad and my family were okay with who I was, I didn't care too much about what everybody else thought of me." She showed a similar trust in the character of God to give her peace of mind when others condemn her. "It doesn't matter who we are [or] what we've done; I think God's grace is still enough for me. Who knows if I'm right or wrong? But come judgment day I'll find out. And, I don't think that anything can turn me away, like it says in the Bible, from the love of Jesus Christ."

When I asked Anita about her current faith, she laughed and said, "It's a roller coaster ride." She added, "I think it's just like anybody else where we have our doubts, we have our fears, just trying to figure out what would God want for us in our life, and trying to do that, trying to follow that path that he created for us. . . . All I want and all I need is just a relationship with God and to know I'm on that path that he put in front of me and that I'm trying to do everything that I possibly can to achieve the things that he's called me to."

REJECTION AND CONDEMNATION

While silence keeps people guessing about what would happen if the truth were spoken, blatant rejection makes it definitive. Experiences of parental rejection among my participants were common, although they varied in severity. When parents learn that their child is gay, their initial reaction is often shock, fear, disappointment, and sadness.[2] Most parents have dreams for their child of a heterosexual marriage and children, so the discovery that a child is gay can feel like a loss of these dreams. When the family holds a religious view that it is wrong to be gay, this conflict is compounded. Conservative Christian parents may feel embarrassed, blamed, or responsible for their child's homosexuality since they are often taught that homosexuality is caused by abuse, overbearing mothers, or weak, ineffective fathers.

The ultimate rejection is termination of the relationship. Four of the women in my study went through a time when they were not even welcome in their parents' homes after coming out or being outed. Two of these, Amy and Kimberly, were homeless as teenagers after getting kicked out of their family homes.

KIMBERLY: "I'LL PROBABLY GO TO HELL"

I met Kimberly during Pride week shortly after I'd completed my master of social work research. She had just started dating a friend of mine, and we were meeting some other friends for brunch before the parade. Kimberly arrived just as we were telling a story of what had happened the night before. We had been walking through a park when a group of Ukrainian college students approached us, asking if we were gay. One man started making vulgar, hip-thrusting gestures and claimed that the Bible says we were sinning. Upon questioning, we learned that these people didn't

2. Davis et al., "Psychological Well Being of Sexual Minority Youth," 1030–41.

actually know anything about the Bible. I wasn't sure how to respond to them since I'd never been judged for my sexuality by people who made their point by thrusting their hips and referencing the Bible. It was bizarre. After hearing this story, Kimberly spoke up in anger, "I hate that, because I *am* a Christian!" She complained that people like that don't reflect her faith, but they lead other people to assume that being Christian and queer means you must hate yourself. I told her about my project and asked her to participate. She quickly agreed.

Kimberly is African American, in her mid-twenties, stands about five foot two, and has long, braided hair. She is calm and principled with a sarcastic sense of humor. She shared her first church-related memory, saying, "The earliest memory [I have] of church is going to a Baptist Church and getting baptized." This memory was not especially meaningful. She laughed as she recalled, "It was scary; that's what I remember! I was like, 'Oh my gosh, I don't want to do this again!'" A few years later, at the age of eight, Kimberly started attending a local suburban charismatic church with her friends. She said, "The people were very welcoming. . . . My friends there knew everybody. It was fun." She went on, "I made a lot of friends there. . . . Church has generally been a positive experience for me, except for the times when my mom has gotten involved with it."

Kimberly laughed at this last thought. She was aware of being attracted to other girls at a young age. She said she knew "officially, when I was ten but probably when I was like four." Seeing my surprise at this young age, she laughed and said, "It makes me sound like I was a perverted kid or I was abused or something, but I wasn't. I just knew."

When I asked Kimberly what kind of messages she heard at home, she said flatly, "That I'll probably go to hell." She explained, "My mom always told me that Scripture about Sodom and Gomorrah. I didn't even know what she was talking about—now I feel like she doesn't know what she was talking about." Kimberly laughed at the absurdity of using the passage about Sodom and Gomorrah to say anything about committed, loving relationships between two people of the same gender.

As she was coming out, Kimberly tried to start conversations with her mom gently. "First I asked her if she knew anyone who was gay, what would [she] do?" Her mom replied, "I wouldn't talk to them, I wouldn't be friends with them." Knowing that her mom would not respond well did not keep Kimberly from coming out, and she wasn't surprised when it went poorly. "At first my mom told me that it was a phase and that she [had] had that phase. That still makes me wonder, like, really? 'You had that phase?' I've never grown out of my phase so I don't know about her." Kimberly laughed and added, "Mom, you should really think about that."

During her teenage years, Kimberly got involved in District 202, a club for LGBTQ youth that, sadly, no longer exists. "It's hard to not come out when you're at the age when you're starting to date and all your friends are dating guys and [you] want to date girls. The only place that I could think of was District 202." Kimberly went there for support, but added, "My mom called the police whenever she would find out that I went there." Her dad, on the other hand, would "sneak" her there. Reflecting on District, she said, "I'm sad that they're not around. They helped me tremendously; I don't even know if I'd be alive today if it weren't for District."

Eventually, the conflict led to Kimberly getting kicked out of the house at age fifteen. She described the importance of her faith at this time: "If I didn't believe in God, I would be dead." She explained, "I've gone through a lot of different things. I don't know if it's because I'm gay and I wasn't able to stay at my mom's or have her involved in my life, but I don't understand not having faith. It's just something I have to have. I can't believe in myself; believing in me isn't anything that's very powerful. Believing in God is something that's beyond me, that's beyond human life."

While her belief in God was always there, as a young adult she put more effort into finding out what it means for her to be lesbian and Christian. "Now I know more about the Bible than I did when I was younger, so I feel more comfortable being a Christian than I did before." In addition to the Bible itself, Kimberly also gathered information from other sources on how biblical texts are interpreted differently. She began to believe that taking a literal, word-for-word interpretation of the Bible is dangerous. "*For the Bible Tells Me So*[3] was a big deal. I still try to get my mom to at least watch the documentary. . . . That helped a lot to learn how contradict[ory] the Bible can be if you take it word for word. I really wouldn't be here today if people took it word for word. I'd be someone's slave somewhere." She laughed as she added, "And you probably would, too," referring to Christians' long history of using the Bible to support slavery, racism, and sexism. Clearly we are not as consistent as we'd like to think we are in determining what is biblical and what is not.

---

3. A 2007 documentary about homosexuality, which includes different biblical interpretations. Karslake, *For the Bible Tells Me So.*

Kimberly had some challenges connecting with other LGBTQ people around issues of faith. She said: "That's a hard thing, being gay and in a community that gets shunned from different religions." She added, "I don't know if I believe that I'm religious. I feel like religious is really really bookish. I believe in God and I feel like He's in me. I feel like He's in you, and anybody who believes in Him. He is there. He or She or It or whatever you want to call God."

Kimberly wishes there were more places available for her to worship in community, and perhaps to bring her partner. She said, "At first [my girlfriend] told me she doesn't believe in God; then she tells me to pray for her." When these prayers work out, Kimberly tells her, "Seriously, that was God. You cannot say that that was just a coincidence!"

The two have looked for church communities but haven't committed.

> I want to go to church; I make up excuses. I think that's [the] hard part too, finding a Christian nondenominational church that isn't . . . Methodist or Catholic or Lutheran or something where I would fall asleep. Because I wasn't raised in churches where you hold [a] paper, and you say one thing, and the pastor or priest or whatever says one thing, and then everybody else says something else, and you talk back and forth and then we listen. No, I'm used to . . . singing and praising the Lord and then hearing a sermon and then singing and praising and then leaving. (Laughs.) I haven't found anything like that; which sucks.

I'm not aware of many lively or charismatic affirming churches nor many racially diverse affirming churches either. The charismatic movement has always attracted diverse people groups and welcomed those who are marginalized. Still, they remain conservative on issues related to sexuality. Most of the affirming churches I know (in Minnesota at least) are liturgical and are made up of mostly upper middle-class white people over the age of forty-five. These churches do not sound interesting to Kimberly or many others who enjoy an energetic worship service.

Since coming out, building her own life, and finding a strong network of support, Kimberly reports feeling like she is in a good place with her faith. She described the changes to her beliefs about God over the years. "The God that I thought that I knew when I was younger was a judgmental, hateful, damning-a-lot-of-people-to-hell God. But now the God that I know has a sense of humor and is less restricted to certain people—the people that are getting married and have children and [are] mostly white people (because the churches I went to, they were predominantly white)." The messages she picked up at her church were not just about gay people, but about racial minorities, gender differences, and the nature of God. She began to see that God is more loving and inclusive than are the Christians she knew.

Kimberly felt some loneliness in that she doesn't know many other queer Christians. She said, "It sucks but I don't have a problem with it. It sucks for other people that don't believe in God, that's how I feel. I think eventually there will be more people, especially if this amendment [proposed in the 2012 election to change the state constitution to limit marriage to one man and one woman] doesn't pass and people are able to get married and then have some part of God involved in what they're doing." The amendment did not pass, and marriage was legalized in Minnesota just six months later. Kimberly's hope is that more LGBTQ people are able to feel welcome in faith communities after developments like this.

PREACHING ABOUT THE "SIN" OF HOMOSEXUALITY

More and more Christian denominations are moving towards affirming and inclusive policies. Still, far too many churches have created cultures of silence or of hostility towards queer people, creating environments that allow for mocking, condemning, scapegoating, and defaming LGBTQ people.

I feel somewhat lucky that I was not involved in evangelical communities as a child. My Catholic culture of silence about sexuality had its drawbacks, but it protected me from the hostility that permeates so many other churches. I didn't grow up with my fellow church members openly mocking gay people or showing disgust for them. I did encounter both of these in the evangelical communities of my adulthood. The actions of these Christians always bothered me. I never understood how they could justify making fun of gay people, feeling secure in their own judgments, and certain that no one in their own community could be "one of them." The mocking came from people who were warm, loving, and generous in so many other ways. I didn't get it.

In my experience, leaders and pastors who formally spoke on the subject of homosexuality tried to be sensitive as they taught that same-sex attractions are the result of sin entering the world. They used terms like "brokenness" and "fallen nature." There was typically a disclaimer that "their sin is not worse than anyone else's," but the jokes, veiled disgust, and policies of exclusion suggested they believed otherwise. Of the eleven people I interviewed, seven reported hearing clear messages about the "sin" of homosexuality from the pulpit of their own church. They heard things like "homosexuality is a sickness," "you are going to hell," "you can't stay here," and "it's disgusting." A few even saw church leaders mocking gay people and promoting fear and hatred as part of the sermon.

Churches have tremendous power to communicate acceptance and love, or to teach condemnation and shame. Participants' experiences spoke to me about how important their churches have been to them, how much they were affected by church teachings, and how much they suffered as they tried to fit in or live up to the church's expectations.

3

Messages: Ex-gay Ministries

REPARATIVE THERAPY

SOME OF THE MOST prolific distributors of misinformation about LGBTQ people have been ex-gay ministries and promoters of reparative therapy. Reparative therapy is a term used to describe any method designed to help people reduce or eliminate their same-sex attractions. The goal is for people to avoid same-gender sexual encounters, fantasies, or pornographic materials and to build heterosexual interests. The methods of these groups have varied widely, from individual counseling, to "healing prayer," to exorcism, to aversion therapy (using electric shocks or other painful methods in an attempt to discourage homosexual arousal). All the ministries claimed to offer reorientation, or at least a reduction in same-sex attractions through their spiritual programs.

Before the recent demise of the most influential reparative therapy organization, reparative therapy groups had been the evangelical church's main source of information about homosexuality. Sadly, the content of their message is both disparaging and inaccurate. Their teachings slander the queer community by portraying queer people as amoral, against God, unhappy, and unhealthy. They have misinformed the Christian church about the results of their methods, claiming that a change in orientation is available if people would just adhere to their programs.

Central to the message of ex-gay groups is their teachings about the causes of homosexuality. Andrew Comiskey, one famous ex-gay leader, wrote, "When understood in the context of a fallen, broken world, heterosexual development is subject to blockage. Homosexuality is one expression of 'getting stuck' along the way to becoming a mature, heterosexual adult."[1] The message of inherent inferiority is clear. Ex-gay groups have promoted their beliefs that children become gay because of bad parenting and traumatic childhood experiences. They cite reasons like physical abuse, sexual abuse, absent fathers, overbearing mothers, neglect, and peer rejection. There is no reputable evidence to support these claims, but these groups hold on to them with a firm grasp.

Reparative therapy has been renounced as ineffective and harmful by professional organizations including the World Health Organization, the American Psychiatric Association, the American Psychological Association, the National Association of Social Workers, the American Academy of Pediatrics, the American Medical Association, and more.[2] Professional Christian counselors rarely offer this therapy and do not typically advertise it if they do. Insurance companies are not interested in paying for treatment that (1) has no empirical research to support its use; (2) claims to treat a condition that is not considered a disorder or a threat to one's health; and (3) is considered unethical by professional licensing boards. For these reasons and others, reparative therapy often stays in the hands of nonprofessional laity (untrained in providing counsel) or those who do not subscribe to their own profession's ethical practices. Recently, California and New Jersey have banned the use of reparative therapy in service to minors.[3]

Several of my participants reported a time when they tried to change their orientation, or hoped that it would "go away," but only one participant went through professional Christian counseling for reparative therapy. Her story highlights how the church was responsible for instilling shame and promoting false hope in her and others.

LAURIE: "TAKE EVERY THOUGHT CAPTIVE"

When I started my research project, several people told me, "You have to talk to Laurie!" She is a pillar of the local gay community, an advocate, and

1. Comiskey, *Pursuing Sexual Wholeness*, 45.
2. Just the Facts Coalition, *Just the Facts*, 6–9.
3. Editorial Board, "Banning a Pseudo-Therapy," SR10.

an ordained minister in the United Church of Christ. She is forty-eight years old and has been deeply committed to faith communities for most of her life. She was happy to take part in an interview, so we met for coffee and gelato in the suburbs. Prior to coming out, she was very involved in a local charismatic mega-church, did mission work in Germany, and attended a conservative Bible college. She spent years trying to change her orientation before exploring other options.

Laurie grew up Catholic but found herself looking into other Christian denominations when she didn't feel like peers at her church shared her interest in faith. Through school she was able to find friends who also took an interest in spiritual things. "When I got to high school, I met some friends that were interested in faith, so we started our own Bible study. It was fairly ecumenical, mostly Lutheran and Catholic, but there were some other denominations wrapped in there. One of the [people] that [was] involved was a woman who went to [a charismatic] church. We were very curious about all that because she was at the 'wild church.'"

When Laurie visited this "wild" church, she was enamored by the passionate worship of a young and vibrant community. "My first experience, there were sixty or seventy kids in the front row having a good time, worshiping God. The music was loud, and the music was fun. . . . I got involved in the youth group [of] 300 kids. It was Friday night, live bands, everybody was, 'Yay Jesus,' and I loved it. I got very involved in what was going on there and soon got involved in the leadership of the ministry."

She caught the energy of the large worship gatherings, made friends, and felt connected to the mission of the church. These experiences were transformative. Soon she spent most of her free time at the church. "I was there every day that the door was open, which was six out of seven days a week. It got so bad that I could never just go to a family event without either coming late from church or going early to get to something at church."

The pastors and community members made their views on homosexuality very clear. "I heard very consistently from the pulpit, any example of someone who is a sinner or sinful or bad—the epitome of the example was usually a gay person." She spoke with sadness about how she came to believe the things they taught about gay people. "One of the beliefs that I took in was that gay people are so contagious, so dangerous, and so cunning, that if you have a gay person in your life, if you have any temptation by them, you need to drive them away. You need to [have a] 'shake the dust off your feet' kind of mentality. You have to let them go and shun them in order to help them understand how bad their behavior is." These views affected both her sense of self and her ability to love other gay Christians.

I'm struck by the impact of Laurie's new church's teachings, which created shame and guilt that didn't exist for her before she joined. Prior to her involvement in this church, she didn't have strong beliefs about what it meant to be gay. She recalled her first awareness of her same-gender attractions. "My first experience was when I was about fourteen. [I] kissed my first boy, the neighbor next door. I was so curious about it, so exhilarated by it that I told this female friend in the neighborhood and she was like, 'Come on let's do it, let's do it.'"

Laurie laughed as she added, "I got further with her that day than I did with him the day before." She went on, "I didn't have any shame or guilt around it, and I didn't think anything of it. To me, love was love."

Not long after this, she met a new friend at school whom she described as her "first real love." She said, "A young woman named Naomi just enthralled me. [The] first day I saw her—I can still see it in my mind thirty-five years later—she walked into the band room, and I saw and I said, 'Oh my God, I think I'm in love!' For the next three years I pursued a close friendship with her because I felt these feelings."

It was about the same time that Laurie started attending the new church where the "sin" of homosexuality was taught frequently. She didn't associate these teachings with the fondness she felt toward her friend. "I had a disconnect; [I thought,] 'I'm not gay just because I love Naomi.' You know? I didn't equate the two . . . because, in my mind, the idea of someone who was gay was promiscuous, sex driven, a nymphomaniac, [or] somebody who preyed on innocent people. I [imagined] a very dark experience, and yet my feelings for Naomi were very warm, loving, and caring."

At first, she compartmentalized her own experience, saying, "The way I feel about Naomi is okay, but gay people are bad." It wasn't until years later that she began to make the connection that her feelings for other women were, in fact, romantic interest.

Inner conflict escalated when she was nineteen, on a mission trip in Europe. "I had these sexual attractions towards other women in our church that I didn't know quite what to do with. I would fight against them and really tried to figure out how to stop it." Despite trying to repress her attractions, she felt "this mix of deep love and care for people that meant a lot to me and a real deep shame and guilt about what I was feeling to begin with." It became a pattern for her of falling for other women in her community.

"But it wasn't like I was seeking it out. I would just start to feel close and feel an affinity towards that person, and then go, 'Whoa, wait a second . . . there's those feelings again, I don't like those feelings, those feelings are bad. . . . I'm going to push this person away so I don't have those feelings.'"

After her mission trip, she returned to her old church and enrolled in Bible college. She began to focus more heavily on trying to change her orientation. "I would be often up on the altar praying and asking God to take this away and please stop this. I eventually started going to counseling with my pastor to try to find help. I even went to a professional counselor because [the pastor] felt there wasn't enough he could do."

Laurie described the futility of her experience of seeing a professional Christian counselor to try to change her orientation.

> The only thing that he did was talk about self-discipline. The only advice he had was, "You need to take every thought captive." That was his corner Scripture. He gave me books about self-control, and mind control, and discipline to try to help me. I stopped going to him after about four or five months because I felt very bad every time I went there, even though he was very compassionate. I felt very bad and I felt very dirty. I couldn't, as hard as I tried, I felt like I could never fully overcome it. There'd be good times and bad times and I started feeling like I was in a yoyo pattern, where I'd be up-and-down, up-and-down, up-and-down. I was always afraid that somebody would look at me and figure me out. That never seemed to go away. I'd suppress it for a while and then it would come out, and then I felt like it was coming out sideways.
>
> One of the patterns that I got myself into is that the moment I started to feel attraction towards another woman I would start to push them away. I found myself isolating from any close friend-ships with women because I was afraid that if I got too close, something would happen—I would lose control or maybe they would reciprocate—and I don't want them to reciprocate because I don't want to know that this is okay.

During this time, Laurie felt so hopeless that she described herself as "a ship lost at sea without a compass."

Things seemed to get worse before they got better. While Laurie was still seeing the counselor, her best friend, Matt, told her that he was gay. She recalled her response: "'Oh, shit,' I thought, 'Why do you have to be gay?' It crushed me, it really crushed me. I didn't know what [to do]. I felt I had to push him away. I had to drive him away because he was going to become a stumbling block for me."

She said to him, "I don't think I can be your friend anymore." She didn't understand how he could be gay and still call himself a Christian. She ended the friendship both to communicate her disapproval and to escape her fear that she would follow the same path. Out of her fear and concern, she asked a friend in her dorm to pray with her that Matt would repent. "After several weeks of praying for Matt I said, 'One of the reasons why this is important to me is that I wrestle with these things too. I'm afraid if he doesn't turn back, what's it gonna do to me?'"

Laurie's friend was apparently scared too. "She promptly turned around and told the Dean of Women, who called me into the office the next day. I was on the honors list; I've never been in the Dean's office. There was no reason that I'd be called into the dean of women's office. I went to my friend and I said, 'What's going on? Is there something you want to tell me?'"

Her friend was defensive and said, "No. I don't know why she's calling you; I have no idea."

Laurie knew better. "I knew she knew why; I had this deep gut sense." She confronted this friend, saying, "You just turned me in! And she's gonna call me on the carpet!"

Her friend continued to deny it, but Laurie, of course, was right. "This was the irony: it was during this time that I felt the strongest in overcoming my tendencies. I felt the most attuned and that I was actually maybe getting the upper hand on this. . . . I felt very much in control, my counselor was working, everything was jiving. And [the dean] told me this, 'Others have pointed you out to me. Even some of the teachers have questioned whether or not you are gay by the way you are—by the way you dress or the way you talk or walk.'"

Laurie was shocked.

> It floored me! Even if there's nothing going on in my life, I can still be perceived as gay. This is ridiculous! And so, like usual, I drove everybody away. I stopped going to my counseling. I stopped talking to my pastor about it, and I literally submarined. I decided, "I am not going to tell anybody. I'm not going to deal with this with anybody." I'm submarining it all. It put me into a deep depression, where I was up and down and struggling very much—very isolated, very alone. And, in the depths of that [saying], "I'm in control over this and I'm still accused of being gay even though

I'm not!" In my head being gay meant that you're acting on it, and I wasn't acting on it.

Laurie started to rethink her theology about same-gender relationships. After being betrayed by a friend, suspected by teachers, and called into the dean's office as if she had done something wrong—all while she was celibate and trying to change her orientation—she dropped her hope of ever living up to the church's heterosexual ideal. "Matt's coming out was the beginning of a turning point for me because [I felt] dissonance [between him and] my preconceived notion of what a homosexual was. He wasn't a sex maniac, [but a] very faithful guy, spiritually attuned, a kindred spirit for me, a very godly person, and very compassionate, and there was so much that didn't make sense. Like, 'How can you be so Christian? How can you be such a faithful person and be gay? That doesn't make sense. You can't do that.'"

I asked Laurie what it was that eventually led her to change her views about homosexuality. "The sheer frustration that I could never overcome this, I could never purge this from my life; I could never become straight," she said. "The slow, growing realization that that's not possible." She asked herself, "Do I want to live a celibate, gay, closeted life and be miserable? Or, do I want to come out and see if I can make that world a life for me?" She added that she realized "where I was at spiritually was not healthy and that something was amiss. What was amiss was the false theology that I had bought into, believing that gay people are evil and going to hell, that if I'm gay then I'm going to hell. No matter how much I love Jesus, I'm going to hell."

As Laurie continued to wrestle with these questions, she critically examined her own faith, health, and happiness: "Real, true, authentic Christianity means peace. Salvation is another term for peace in Hebrew, and so, if I'm truly saved then peace should be prevalent in my life. And yet I am void of peace. . . . I'm not in harmony with God; there's no wholeness." Laurie started on a new journey of seeking out truth for herself. As she came to terms with her own unhappiness, she thought, "Something is not lining up here and I don't know where it is. I've been living up to everybody else's expectations, and they're telling me what the Bible says about these things. It's time for me to dig in and figure this out for myself. I'd taken all kinds of Bible study and exegesis work, learning how to do hermeneutics and things like that. I had all the tools in my hands; I'd been working with them for three years. I knew what to do, and so I started digging in."

As she studied, she came to a new understanding of biblical texts. "I came to the conclusion scripturally: there's no grounds, there's no clear grounds to say that homosexuality is a sin of God and a sin worthy of ostracism from the faith. And, God's will for me is to be healthy and whole and loved and cared for, and community and relationships are key."

Laurie went through a long process of discerning what the Bible really said and what was healthy for her. She remained committed to her faith and to following the Bible as she understood it. "It was never an issue of whether or not I was a Christian. I never went through that phase where it was like, 'I'm a terrible sinner.' I was always a very faithful Christian. My wrestling was, 'How is it possible to integrate these two worlds?' That's where I struggled the most. For a long time I asked the question, 'Is it possible to even integrate these two things? Do I have to choose one or the other?' I longed for that space where I could find some kind of happy medium."

Since all of her friends and classmates were conservative Christians, she needed to make a purposeful effort to seek out spaces in which she could integrate her faith and sexuality. "From the age of fourteen until twenty-seven I lived a celibate, Christian, anti-gay, reparative therapy–type environment in different forms and different ways. I knew that I couldn't immediately come out, otherwise I'd jeopardize all my schooling." She knew she could have been kicked out of Bible college during her final semester for going public about being gay. In addition, she knew she would lose all of her friends, her church, and maybe her family. Being proactive, she decided, "I need to develop a safety net of support, a new faith community from which I can fall into and figure out where I'm going."

Laurie came up with a rather clever way to find affirming communities while she was still closeted (and under suspicion) at Bible college.

> From February until May I worked on my senior paper around 'how to evangelize the homosexual.' My degree was in crosscultural studies; anthropology mixed with the gospel was the big part of the theology of missions. So I thought, 'I will perceive the gay culture as a subculture. They see themselves as a subculture, so I need to approach them like a subculture of society [to] which I minister.' That was the premise of my paper, but it gave me cover to research gay-friendly congregations and see how different denominations addressed the issue of homosexuality. So I found anti-gay, reparative therapy–type environments; I found quasi-welcoming congregations like the Methodists (at the time); I found the gay church; I found the UCC. I found all these different

denominations, and I researched how they relate to homosexuals and what's their theology about gay people. My opening line of the paper is, 'This is not a paper to argue theological proof about whether or not being gay is against God's will. The premise of this paper is how to most effectively reach out to the gay community with the gospel of Jesus Christ by perceiving them and treating them as a subculture as they see themselves.' I got a B+ on it. I had to do an oral defense. And, they let me graduate, which shocked the hell out of me.

Laurie's story makes me smile. After being called into the dean of women's office and being told that "some professors" had pointed her out as a possible lesbian, she had the guts to write her senior paper on reaching the gay community with the gospel in a culturally relevant way. Writing this paper led her to find the support she needed. "I found segments of the gay community where I didn't feel threatened. I didn't go to the bar scene right away. . . . I found some gay-friendly churches. I found a gay social and support group at the Catholic Church, so I actually went back to the Catholic Church for a little while right after I came out because it was a community of people that got me."

Once she found a network of support and graduated from college, she prepared to come out at her church of over ten years. She said, "I was getting ready to leave the church and my one ray of hope was: if the pastor supports me or at least is willing to allow me to be in ministry, then maybe I'm okay and maybe I can make this happen." She set up an appointment to meet with the pastor. "In that conversation I said, 'I want to stay in ministry at the church.' For me, to be a Christian is to be in ministry, and to be in ministry means I'm teaching. And he's like, 'No you can't. You can't be in ministry. You can come and be in worship; you can be involved in the church, but you can't be involved with the kids and you can't be involved in leadership as long as you say that you're going to actively pursue your gay identity.'"

Laurie responded firmly, "Then this is the last day I'm in this church." She walked away with her head held high and her heart hurting.

After being told she could no longer be in ministry at her beloved church, she stepped away from faith communities for a while. "One of the things that helped me through that phase was separating my relationship with God from a faith community, and putting that sense of call up on a shelf, and that need for community off to the side, and just focusing on: I love God, I believe in God, and I'm fine."

She eventually found her way to a new church, but the separation seemed to be an important step. "I still had a very strong sense of calling to evangelism, missions, some type of ministry, but I thought, 'I've got to put this on hold. God, I've gotta put this up here [on the shelf], and when you think I'm ready to take it on again, bring it!' But I can't figure out in my little head how [it's] gonna be possible for me to be gay, out, and a Christian—and in ministry. That kind of reconstruction took a while."

Less than a year after leaving her church, a chance meeting led her to a new community that was able to challenge her intellectually and encourage her spiritual growth. She was having a spiritual conversation with a friend at a local LGBTQ bookstore when their conversation was overheard by a professor at United Theological Seminary. This stranger approached them and said, "You guys are really into this." After some conversation the professor invited her to look into attending seminary at United.

Laurie visited the school, talked to professors, and sat in on a class. She began to feel clarity about her next step. She described hearing an "echo" while at UTS, which said to her, "This is where you need to go; this is where you need to be."

Laurie enrolled right away and found her time there to be very helpful. She said:

> I wouldn't be able to integrate those two worlds at just a congregation because the congregations that I had been visiting were not [at] the spiritual depth, theological depth that I was used to. They were welcoming and friendly places that were really saccharine in some ways. I thought, "This is where I can get down and wrestle in the mud on this. I can really get into this!" And my first class was Homosexuality and the Church. So I jumped into the deep end—big time! I got liberation theology, and I really did bounce off the walls. I was a fundamentalist in a progressive school—it was crazy.

Despite feeling like a bit of an outsider, she also felt like it was the perfect place for her to ask questions and study biblical texts for answers. "People were there to support me. They didn't always like what I had to say because I was so conservative, but they gave me latitude. I started to settle into a groove; I started to transform theologically. I still don't think I'm as progressive as people would like me to be, but it was a good transition. And it was a place where I could really start to integrate and become proud of being gay and proud of being Christian. That was important to me."

Laurie finally found a place where she was challenged to study the Bible in a new light. She needed the spiritual depth of seminary to work out her own questions, even if that meant standing out as the fundamentalist among progressives. Her studies and the welcome of this community allowed her to feel, for the first time, that she had an integrated life.

Now, she is a minister in the United Church of Christ. She said of this community, "I feel very spiritually grounded when I'm there. It's a rich spiritual community." She still considers herself more conservative than some of her community members and challenges them to think about evangelism in new ways that are welcoming rather than off-putting. She and others in her community have been angered by the actions of the evangelical church and have wrestled with sharing the name "Christian."

> I still feel very jaded by the evangelical church. I will go through phases where I don't even want to call myself a Christian. I cringe when somebody says that to me, and I'm like, "No, no, no, I'm not that kind of Christian." I can get very defensive. I cringe at what goes on in the news when they talked about "the Christians." "The Christians hate gay people," and "the Christians do this," "Christianity is this way." . . . Michelle Bachmann does not represent the Christian church; she represents the anti-Christian church, you know?

Despite being turned off by certain Christians, Laurie has experienced significant personal and spiritual growth in the years since she came out.

> I think I have a much richer spirituality, that it's more personal. I never used to have a strong devotional life. Even in all the years it was: when I'm in trouble, I'm going to pray; when I'm not in trouble, "Forget you God, I'm fine." It was very much this outward expression of faith. Now it's much more integrated where I cherish the three hours in the morning that I have to be alone, and I do whatever I want. I pray, I read scripture, I meditate, I do body stretches, I read my email. I do whatever I want, but it's my time— my time with God and being attuned to that.

I ended each of the interviews by asking participants if their view of God had changed. Laurie responded, "Not a lot," then added, "I think my view of the church has changed a hell of a lot more." She explained:

> I have always seen God as an extremely loving, caring, and compassionate being. I think I appreciate God's grace much more today than I ever did. I can't say that I fully understand grace today,

but my understanding of grace back then was, "you use that term but I don't get it." Today, I think I have a better handle on it. I get frustrated with myself when I can't show that same grace to somebody else. I am certainly not caught up in the legalism that I once was—that's probably the biggest area. It walks hand-in-hand with the grace concept: God really does not get hung up on what you do or do not do. He really could give a shit. . . . He could. . . . *She could* . . . say, "I don't care how many things you do or do not do. I don't care if you go dancing. I don't care if you drink. I really don't care if you're swearing, I really don't care. All that I care about is: Are you being a loving person? Are you emulating the essence of who I am, which is, and only is: love."

Laurie has earned a reputation of living out her ideals. She is a well-known and well-loved example of Christian leadership in the LGBTQ community. I look at her story, and I thank God that her reparative therapy was a complete failure. I'm just sorry she had to suffer so much to get where she is today. She has used her story and her pain to speak to others and to bring healing.

My Ex-gay Story

My first exposure to the claims of ex-gay ministries was during my junior year of college. My campus Christian group hung posters throughout the student union, claiming "Change Is Possible" for gay people. They referenced the testimonies of people who claimed that God had changed them from gay to straight. The stories were dramatic, telling how people escaped from drug addiction, sex addiction, abusive relationships, and other terrible situations. The stories were not like mine; I had a loving family and a rather sheltered, suburban existence. I hadn't ever been in a relationship with a woman. Still, I was curious about their claims. That year I hid in the back of the campus computer labs as I searched for online testimonies of "ex-gay" people. I crept around the Christian bookstore and smuggled my ex-gay purchases through the aisles and up to the cashier. I read books about "escaping" homosexuality from several different authors. While these books presented information in a manner that was intended to be kind and loving, they conveyed a great deal of shame and painted gay people as miserable and unhealthy.

After my campus group hung the "Change Is Possible" posters, The 10% Society (named after the inaccurate statistic that 10 percent of the population is gay) hosted a panel discussion, which included various local affirming clergy. They discussed how Old and New Testament passages have been misinterpreted and that the Bible does not clearly condemn same-gender relationships. We'd been encouraged to attend this forum in order to hear what these "false teachers" were saying. I attended the forum, not to gather evidence against them but to see if they could convince me that it was okay to be gay. As I listened, I thought they were taking liberties with the Bible, and I was not able to agree with them. I thought they were twisting passages around in order to say what they wanted. I left the forum frustrated and saddened. I concluded once again that the truth was a hard pill to swallow—so I swallowed the pill and continued to believe that same-gender relationships were wrong.

Looking back, I wonder what led me to believe the claims of ex-gay books when I didn't grow up with strong messages about homosexuality being sinful (or fixable). My biggest motivator was that I did not want to give up my faith. By this time, my closest friends were part of my campus Christian group. Ex-gay materials provided some hope that I could stay in community *and* find a lifelong partner. I was skeptical of their claims. Still, I wanted to believe that I could be made "normal." They claimed that normal could be achieved by addressing the roots of my homosexuality.

I never could relate to the claims that bad parenting causes homosexuality. I'd had a good relationship with my mom and dad, and I never once doubted their love for me. The only one of the possible causes that I couldn't dismiss was the experience of sexual abuse. Abuse is inherently damaging, so it was not hard for me to believe that abuse left me with an unhealthy sexuality.

The summer before reading ex-gay books, I had started facing my own memories of sexual abuse. It was something I had put out of my mind for a very long time. I always knew that *something* had happened with a friend of the family when I was quite young, but my memories were foggy and incomplete and easily dismissed. The "easily dismissed" part changed while I was on a summer mission project in Latvia. After coming across a small bit of information about the impact of sexual abuse, I decided to tell a friend what had happened to me. I thought that telling someone would be like a load off my mind and that I could then put it all behind me. Instead, I was nauseous for days. I was thrown into confusion, anger, and depression that lasted the next nine months. During this time I begged God to help me. I had never experienced such a low before. I had been told that becoming a Christian makes you happier and more fulfilled—that you are automatically happier than those who don't know Jesus—but I felt worse than ever. I felt ostracized from my community, which didn't understand what was going on with me. The community did not know how to address the pain that its own members might be experiencing, and I didn't know how to ask for help. During that year I began a habit of cutting myself that continued (on and off) for the next ten years. I felt incredibly alone.

For me, cutting was a way to calm myself when I was feeling terrible. There were times when I felt a cloud of darkness, anger, and self-hatred come over me. I felt crushed by these emotions, but they were still, strangely, out of reach. It was a miserable fog; I couldn't cry, I couldn't name it, and I couldn't figure out what was wrong. Since my memory of the abuse was vague and incomplete, I kept telling myself that what happened shouldn't bother me so much. When I told myself I was making a big deal out of nothing, cutting made my pain seem real and valid. After seeing blood, I could breathe again.

Six months into my depression I sought out a Christian counselor. As I learned to allow myself to feel emotions instead of telling myself how I should feel, my depression lifted, and I began to feel like I was functional again—jaded, but functional. I didn't tell my counselor about the cutting or being attracted to women; still, it was a helpful step out of my darkness. As I slowly emerged from my depression, I began to more fully acknowledge that I was attracted to women. This was not good news.

THE DANGERS OF DISCUSSING SEXUAL ABUSE

I wrestled with whether or not I should include this part of my own story. Since their inception, ex-gay ministries have claimed that sexual abuse is a major cause of homosexuality. They say that both abuse and homosexuality can be fully healed through their programs, practicing spiritual disciplines, and following God. I know that some will claim that abuse is why I'm lesbian, or they will use this information to make their point that being attracted to women is inherantly unhealthy. Still, I include this part of my story for several reasons.

First, reparative therapies have claimed that for those who have experienced abuse, healing from that abuse will lead to more heterosexual interests and "healthy" relating to the opposite sex. For me, it's true that addressing past abuse has led to more meaningful relationships with both men and women. Still, the more I worked through past abuse, the more I've been able to see sexuality as a whole as a good thing. Healing from sexual abuse did not lead me to become any straighter. Instead, it made me aware of the many ways I have discredited my own thoughts, emotions, and perceptions, telling myself that I am probably wrong for feeling the way I do. Healing is an ongoing process that has meant trusting myself again and letting go of the shame connected to how I feel.

Second, I refuse to believe that coming out as lesbian means I have to go back into hiding about other things. I've come to love living with absolutely nothing to hide. Recovery catch phrases like "our secrets keep us sick" have been ingrained in my head, and I believe them. Hiding has promoted shame in my life, and I don't want to go back there.

Most of the testimonies I read of women in ex-gay ministries included a history of sexual abuse. Later, I was surprised to learn that only 32 percent of lesbian women report sexual abuse in their history.[4] I'm not saying that 32 percent is a small number, but the materials I'd read had claimed "nearly all" of the women seen by ex-gay ministries had an abuse history. Perhaps ex-gay ministries were only attracting women who were predisposed to believing their orientation was a result of the damage from abuse and needed healing.

Ex-gay ministries have argued that the higher prevalence of abuse histories among LGBTQ people supports their claim that abuse is one cause of a homosexual orientation—that abuse turns people gay. Social science researchers have suggested an alternative: being LGBTQ increases one's risk of being targeted for abuse. Some studies have shown that sexual minority adolescents are at a greater risk of experiencing sexual and physical abuse than sexual nonminorities. Friedman and colleagues found: "Compared with sexual nonminority adolescents, sexual minority adolescents were on average 2.9 times more likely . . . to report childhood sexual abuse. The mean of the absolute prevalence was 40.4% for bisexual females, 32.1%, for lesbian females, and 16.9% for heterosexual females. The mean of the absolute prevalence was 24.5% for bisexual males, 21.2% for gay males, and 4.64% for heterosexual males."[5]

They conclude that being gay, lesbian, or bisexual puts kids at higher risk of being sexually abused. Perpetrators choose their victims carefully, often choosing kids who are different, isolated, or otherwise unlikely to tell

4. Friedman et al., "Disparities in Childhood Sexual Abuse," 1481–94.

5. Ibid., 1483.

adults. Young gay males seem especially vulnerable to these predators. Girls who are tomboys may also be easily targeted. Some continue to argue that being abused leads people to become gay, but this has certainly not been proven. The majority of queer women (and men) have never experienced sexual abuse and do not fit this description promoted by ex-gay ministries.

WHATEVER THE CAUSE, THERE IS NO "CURE"

Whatever it is that caused us to be gay, here we are. Sexuality is incredibly complex and is influenced by many factors. Even if certain life experiences could tip the Kinsey scale slightly in one direction or the other, there's no reason to believe those experiences can be undone. Since there is clearly no reputable "treatment" for those who want to change their orientation (and most queer people don't want to change), maybe we, as Christians, could accept each other's orientation and celebrate each other's ability to find healthy, life-giving relationships. And maybe we can stop using a person's most painful life experiences to try to prove that they are damaged.

There are so many human traits that cannot be clearly defined as either "born this way" or shaped by the environment. The "nature versus nurture" debate is carried into all realms of human behavior. For example, I have identical twin nephews. They share the same genes, but one is left-handed and one is ambidextrously right-handed. Genes don't tell the whole story of hand preference, neither does societal pressure to conform to the right-handed majority. There was a time when left-handed people were demonized, and children were forced to use their right hand to conform to the majority. Now we rightly see this practice as abusive. The question of whether or not a person is born left-handed is completely irrelevant. They are left-handed now.

To carry this analogy even further, I once worked with a janitor whose right arm had been amputated at the elbow. His resulting left-handedness became such a part of his identity that he took on the nickname Lefty. I have no idea what his given name was; he was Lefty to all who knew him at work. He was always smiling and joking with the people he encountered and seemed to have made a good life after his "natural" tendency towards right-handedness was taken. Some extreme Christians might say that God could restore Lefty's right arm, but I can't imagine who. It seems to me that Christians who claim that a person's heterosexuality can be restored after abuse might as well be praying that God would grow Lefty a new right arm.

Who would tell Lefty that his identity is wrapped up in his damaged self and that he should not identify as left-handed because that is not how God made him? I don't know any Christians who would require this of him. Some things cannot be undone.

Still, I'm uncomfortable with this analogy. I don't believe that abuse was an amputation of my natural heterosexual self. I think I would be gay even if the abuse never happened—I believe I would have come out much sooner and probably avoided ex-gay ministries all together. Since many Christians have claimed that sexual abuse is a major cause of homosexuality, I'm exploring: what if it were true for *some* people? I'm not convinced it is, but even if it were true, why couldn't we celebrate a person's ability to find and express love after abuse as tremendously adaptive and resilient?

TWO APOLOGIES

Dr. Robert Spitzer

There have been a few events in recent years that give me hope that reparative therapy is losing any credibility it once had in evangelical circles. One such event was the apology of Dr. Robert Spitzer. Dr. Spitzer was one of the most influential psychiatrists in the efforts to get homosexuality removed from the list of mental disorders in the *Diagnostic and Statistical Manual* (DSM). When gay rights advocates started to challenge psychiatry's classification of homosexuality as a mental disorder, Spitzer took the time to hear their stories and their reasons for protest. After hearing them out, he became a strong advocate for the removal of homosexuality from the DSM.[6] He and others argued that mental disorders are defined by marked distress and impairment and that while homosexuality may be associated with higher risk of mental illnesses, it does not, it itself, cause distress or impairment. Eventually, the American Psychiatric Association voted with Spitzer, and homosexuality was removed from the DSM in 1973.[7]

About twenty-five years after the changes to the DSM, Spitzer was approached by a group of people who were angry with psychiatry's denial of their existence and their stories. An ex-gay movement was on the rise, and they wanted the world of psychiatry to take note. Spitzer showed an interest in hearing from the minority voice once again. He listened to their

6. Carey, "Psychiatry Giant Sorry," A1.

7. APA, *Appropriate Therapeutic Responses*, 23.

stories and decided to conduct a study. He recruited two hundred participants who claimed to have benefitted from ex-gay ministries to take part in phone interviews. The participants included staff members of organizations like Exodus International, NARTH (National Association for the Research and Therapy of Homosexuals), and other reparative therapy groups. The study was not random but solicited volunteers who wanted to take part in a study that would prove the efficacy of treatment. Some of his interview subjects claimed that they had experienced a change in orientation. Spitzer concluded that change may be possible for a few "highly motivated individuals."

Spitzer's intent was to explore the possibility that change was possible for people who wanted to change their orientation from gay to straight. He had no idea how his research would be used and misused to promote an agenda that denied equal rights to LGBTQ people. Spitzer went from being a hero in the queer community to being viewed as a traitor. For many years he stood by his study, saying it was not intended to measure effectiveness of any particular intervention but to explore the possibility of change for those who wanted it. Nearly ten years later (May 19, 2012), he recanted his research conclusions and offered an apology to the gay community. He pointed out flaws in the study: using a nonrandomized sample, failing to address reasons participants may misrepresent the change they experienced, and measuring change solely on self-report. His apology stated that the reparative therapy study was his "only professional regret."[8]

Exodus International

In June 2012, Exodus International, the largest ex-gay organization, announced that they would no longer support or endorse therapies aimed at changing a person's sexual orientation. They admitted that these therapies offered a false hope for change and often utilized questionable methods. They disaffiliated with NARTH and many of the practices that some of their affiliates were promoting. They had already dropped their motto, "Change Is Possible," several years earlier, admitting that it offered an unrealistic hope for those who seek to change their orientation, setting them up for disappointment. They also began conversations with the Gay Christian Network, an online organization that seeks to hold respectful dialogue about *all* of the options available to LGBTQ Christians.

8. Carey, "Psychiatry Giant Sorry," A1.

Exodus President, Alan Chambers, spoke out against some of the practices used by those who claimed to be providing reparative therapies. The practices of these former affiliates included aversion therapy, exposing gay people to heterosexual pornography as therapy, and claiming 100 percent "cure" rates. Chambers stated that he could no longer be associated with the deception used by some of these groups. Finally, in June 2013, Exodus International announced that they would be closing their doors. Alan Chambers once again offered a sincere apology for his own actions and those of the organization in promoting false hope, contributing to the defamation of LBGTQ people, and for downplaying the ongoing same-sex attractions of their leaders and poster children.[9]

I found his apology to be sincere. I disagree with his position that acceptable choices for gay and lesbian people are limited to celibacy and heterosexual marriage. I wish he would stop promoting these beliefs to the masses. Still, I would like to remain supportive of those LGBTQ individuals who cannot reconcile same-sex relationships with their religious beliefs. I often need to remind myself of what it felt like to know I was gay and believe that I could not act on my own attractions. My dearest friends are the few who supported me before *and* after I was okay with my lesbian self.

9. Steffan, "Alan Chambers Apologizes," lines 60–133

4

Messages: Media, Politics, and Wider Communities

MEDIA AND NEWS SOURCES

EVEN THOSE WHO HAVE no personal affiliation with Christianity are likely to hear religiously based negative messages about LGBTQ people. These messages are prevalent, saturating news stories, social media, and political campaign advertisements. Famous Christian leaders and Bible-toting politicians have used their media platforms to speak out against the "sin of homosexuality" for decades. They have not only claimed that LGBTQ people are sinful but that we are responsible for the perceived moral decay of the Western world, blaming gay people for natural disasters, disease, acts of terror, and economic decline. *The Advocate* (an LGBT news and commentary magazine) compiled a list of the top ten disasters that are "supposedly our fault." These include Hurricane Katrina, the September 11 attacks, the 2011 tsunami in Japan, and multiple earthquakes in California.[1] These claims might be laughable, but each of these disasters caused senseless deaths from dozens to thousands of innocent people. These leaders obviously have a particular fear or hatred of gay people to place that kind of blame on us.

These few-but-loud leaders have used several biblical passages to back their teaching that homosexuality is especially sinful and a threat to the

---

1. Garcia, "It's All Our Fault!," lines 1–61.

"moral fiber" of our Christian communities. They've persuaded others to believe that the way one interprets the Bible in regard to homosexuality is the defining point on whether or not they are truly Christian.

I didn't ask my participants about messages they heard from media sources as children. The focus of my research was on early messages they heard from the church and family. Still, several talked about the impact of Christian-inspired negative messages that they saw in the news, since these messages are hard to escape.

Gretchen was the only participant who didn't grow up in a religious family. She took an interest in theology and spiritual practices as a teenager in the 1980s. This was in the midst of the AIDS crisis when Christian leaders were claiming the disease was God's judgment on gay people. She remembered TV evangelists saying that "AIDS was God's wrath on the gays and, gays were dying because God hates fags." She described the two vastly different things she was hearing about Christianity.

> You had these books about gnosticism and the origins of Christianity, [which] was all really fascinating. To me, that's what Christianity became. All these other people were just a bunch of politicians that were trying to grab power. They were trying to influence the community by demonizing [gay people] and saying and doing horrible things that, I thought, were leading to the death of innocent people. I had a really hard time reconciling that. But, those things were separate. Delving into theological ideas and concepts—which is what all the great theologians have always done—I loved that! All of these opportunists were bleeding little old ladies out of their retirements, selling books and selling condos, [on] the PTL Club or whatever. It's like, "What is that?" That's not this thing that I'm reading; it's this thing over here that felt to me like something so abhorrent. It infuriated me. While I was in college, it physically made me so angry that I could only talk about it for short periods of time because I would just want to explode.

Gretchen is still affected by these messages, but her reaction is different now. "Sometimes I can't watch TV when I hear some of these people getting up and quacking. I used to get furious, and now it brings me to tears. It breaks my heart."

Thankfully, a lot has changed for LGBTQ people since the 1980s, and public support has risen steadily. In 1999 two-thirds of Americans believed that gay and lesbian couples should not have the same rights as heterosexual couples in regard to marriage; by 2004, 49 percent of Americans "agreed that same-gender couples who enter a civil union should have the same rights as a heterosexual married couple."[2] This is a dramatic shift in just five years. This change has been encouraging; still, with change comes reaction and fear.

Despite many positive changes since the eighties and nineties, public condemnation of LGBTQ people is still common. Most do not go the the extreme of Fred Phelps and his Westborough clan who claim that "God hates fags," but plenty try to wear a kinder facade as they argue that accepting queer people is going against the Bible. In 2010, Marcus Bachmann, therapist and husband of Minnesota senator Michele Bachmann, was interviewed on a Christian radio program where he likened gay teens to barbarians who need to be educated and disciplined.[3] In 2009, another Minnesotan, Baptist preacher John Piper, claimed that the tornado that had ripped through south Minneapolis, destroying homes and small businesses was God's "gentle but firm warning" to the Lutheran Church (ELCA) that they should vote against the ordination of gay pastors.[4]

Ironically, I think statements like these hurt the Christian church more than they hurt the gay community. Rational people are turned off by these messages and increasingly turned off by Christianity, as declining church membership numbers have shown. Comments like Piper's are still infuriating, not just because gay people are scapegoated for any number of problems, but because theses comments paint God as a vengeful monster. These accusations are predictably common. I've come to expect that when something goes wrong in this country, *someone* will blame the gays.

POLITICS

In addition to the messages of blame and condemnation from religious leaders and politicians, political efforts have heightened the tension. Political campaigns and marriage amendments designed to limit marriage to heterosexual couples have drawn out more harmful messages, calling every voting citizen to give their opinion on the validity of same-sex relationships. Social media has provided a forum for each person to share this opinion with the masses. I remember being deeply hurt by Facebook friends (people I care about) who posted their reasons for voting "yes" on

2. Avery et al., "America's Changing Attitudes," 71.

3. Kennedy, "Marcus Bachman," lines 40–46.

4. Piper, "Tornado, Lutherans, and Homosexuality," line 52.

the Minnesota marriage amendment that would deny equal legal protection for same-gender civil unions. Face to face, most people have not found it necessary to tell me that they think I'm sinning, but social media is another story.

I'm not alone in feeling the impact of political tension. When marriage amendments have been proposed in other states, queer people have suffered. Several studies have explored the impact of these amendments. In states where amendments were initiated, lesbian, gay, and bisexual (LGB) people were exposed to significantly more negative messages than LGB people in states that did not have a marriage amendment on the ballot. These messages came in the form of radio or television advertisements, bumper stickers, yard signs, and billboards.[5] These messages came with a cost. During the campaign season, LGB people in states with a marriage amendment on the ballot experienced more depressive symptoms, negative affect, and stress than LGB people in other states.[6] When states have passed these amendments, the discrepancy in health outcomes is even higher.[7]

Minnesota was presented with just such an amendment in 2012. In the year leading up to the election, we were exposed to television commercials and radio ads that argued that same-gender relationships were inferior, a threat to children, and a sign of moral decline. It got ugly. I remember driving in my car and hearing on the radio, "Angry gay protestors want to force this issue on us no matter what."[8] According to this ad, any queer people pushing for the right to marry were "angry gay protesters." I'd never heard such blatantly defamatory messages on my music station before. I remember thinking, "Well, *now* I'm angry!"

The political focus on banning gay marriage has placed the spotlight on gay people, making us a symbol of relativism and hedonism that the Christian world must fight against. Sadly, the Christian morals of importance to many Christians have not included caring for the poor, welcoming the outcast, feeding the hungry, or offering help to those who suffer. For many conservative Christians, standing up for Christian values has come to mean standing against gay people.

Thankfully, that November I celebrated with my friends and family on a very memorable election night when my fellow Minnesotans voted

5. Riggle et al., "Marriage Amendments," 83–84.

6. Ibid., 84.

7. Rostosky et al., "Psychological Reactions," 302.

8. Hawkins, "MN Marriage-amendment."

down the amendment. Six months later the senate passed a marriage equality bill into law that allows legal recognition of same-gender marriages. In the course of one year we went from valid concern that our state would ban gay marriage to celebrating a victory for equal protection. The progress has been encouraging.

WIDER COMMUNITIES

Each of the women I interviewed reported current faith that was important to them. Even so, several spoke about wanting to distance themselves from Christianity because of the predominant messages that Christians don't like gay people. Participants talked about the difficulty they faced in finding other queer people who shared their faith and how they sometimes tried to hide their Christian identity within LGBTQ circles.

The prevalence of Christian-inspired hateful messages have made many LGBTQ people want nothing to do with the church. Queer communities have often reacted by labeling Christians as hateful and ignorant. The reaction is understandable since the most resistance to LGBTQ advocacy and acceptance comes in the name of Christianity, and the Bible is often used as justification for all kinds of mistreatment. These cultural dynamics leave queer Christians with few options for finding places they can bring their whole selves. Those who want to maintain both queer and Christian identities can feel like outsiders among both groups.

During the interviews, some participants spoke to the difficulty they faced being open about their faith within the queer community. Some felt misunderstood for their faith, feared judgment for their involvement in a church, or just kept quiet about their spiritual beliefs. Some felt, for a time, that they really did have to choose between queer or Christian. Laurie came out just after graduating from Bible college. She said, "When I came out as gay, I went into the closet as Christian." She had to work hard at finding gay-friendly faith environments. Kimberly wasn't involved in a church at the time of the interview and had never connected with other queer Christians. She talked about feeling lonely in her faith. "I'm probably the only Christian that I know." She wanted to say to people in the queer community that "there are actually gay people that do believe in God that truly are Christians who don't hate themselves." Her queer friends had apparently associated queer Christianity with self-loathing.

Anita grew up in an evangelical church that offered English and Spanish ministries. Her friends have questioned why she would want to stay involved in church when Christians have promoted such harmful messages. "A lot of my friends who are gay have turned away from their faith because they take one Scripture and say, 'There it is, plain Jane. It says right there that we're sinners.' They take that, and they don't believe that there is a God anymore—that He would create something to be despicable in His eyes." Anita has pointed out others to me, saying things like, "She used to be a super conservative Christian," or "She went to this Bible college." All of these friends were effectively turned off of Christianity.

As I look back on my experiences in the college Christian group, I see that they taught a number of things that I now consider harmful. The expectation that members be a shining example of "the good life" was not realistic. The belief that anyone who hasn't prayed a certain prayer goes to hell alienated me from people I loved. The culture of conformity was stifling. Their teachings about queer people were the most hurtful, causing fear, shame, and a certain resolve that my life would always be a struggle, that it would lack the kind of love and fulfillment that others got to experience.

5

Impact: Identity Conflict and Mental Health Issues

IN REVIEW, NEGATIVE MESSAGES about homosexuality remain hard to escape, stemming from religious environments, political campaigns, and various cultural dynamics that permeate our daily lives. Churches and families, ex-gay ministries, the media, and wider communities have been the bearers of claims that gay people are especially sinful and unhealthy. Next, we'll explore how these messages have affected women who identify as Christian and lesbian or bisexual, leaving them susceptible to all sorts of painful and damaging experiences.

The stories of each of my participants reveal the impact negative messages had on their lives. My group of ten women faced homelessness, family estrangement, ongoing arguments, and even physical assault. They experienced depression, hopelessness, isolation, shame, disordered eating, and thoughts of suicide. It was clear that the "Christian" messages of condemnation caused significant harm to these women and their relationships. The most hidden and sinister repercussions are the ways in which queer women take on beliefs about themselves that are based on the judgment of others, believing that there is something wrong with them or that they are destined for hell no matter what they do.

IDENTITY CONFLICT

For several decades, a small group of researchers have explored concepts related to sexual identity formation among LGBTQ individuals, looking into which factors help young people develop a healthy sense of self. Developmental psychology professor, Ritch Savin-Williams, defines sexual identity as "the term an individual assigns to himself or herself based on the most salient sexual aspects of his or her life—such as sexual attractions, fantasies, desires, behaviors, and relationships. It gives meaning and significance to the configuration of feelings, perceptions, and cognitions that an individual has about the various domains of sexuality in her or his life."[1]

The major difference between sexual orientation and sexual identity is that one's orientation is not chosen, while one's sexual identity is. The act of coming out is a decision to associate with a gay or lesbian sexual identity, based on one's homosexual orientation. This is helpful in understanding the different choices Christians make regarding same-gender relationships. Some may choose to identify as lesbian, gay, bisexual, or queer. Others may choose to identify as someone who experiences same-sex attraction, and others may choose to not identify either way, hoping (perhaps) to change or deny their orientation.

Sexual identity formation is a process. Lesbian identity development often begins in childhood with a sense of being different from one's peers.[2] Typically, in puberty, these girls begin to have an awareness of their attraction to other girls and may or may not experiment in relationships. Lesbian identity does not develop in a vacuum but "alongside and entangled with" other identities, such as spiritual, racial, cultural, and gender identities.[3] Conflict between these developing identities can be difficult to navigate.

Some have proposed that there are four different choices available to people who experience conflict between their sexual and religious identity. These are: rejecting their sexuality, rejecting their religious self, compartmentalizing the two identities, or integrating the identities through an affirming faith.[4] In the stories gathered here, these categories are not always clear cut, but the women often went through different stages as they moved towards integration of their sexual and spiritual selves.

1. Savin-Williams, "Identity Development," 671–89.
2. McCarn and Fassinger, "Revisioning," 522.
3. Shapiro et al., "Conceptualizing," 505.
4. Rodriguez and Ouellette, "Gay and Lesbian Christians," 39–53.

My Story: Trying Not to Be Gay

After college, I tried to avoid thinking much about my own sexual orientation. I moved back to St. Paul, found a job, and rented a house with three friends. At first, this arrangement was fantastic. We all got along well and spent lots of time together. I didn't like my job much, but it didn't matter; it was temporary as I tried to pay down student loans and prepare for a call to the mission field that I was certain would come soon enough.

After a year in the house, the dynamics between roommates turned sour, and I grew uncomfortable there. Meanwhile, I kinda fell in love with one of my roommates. This caused some problems. I met Jenny in college. She and I were both struggling with post-graduation, directionless angst in our searches for careers, churches, and new friends. I began to share with her that I was typically attracted to women. She began to open up to me about a relationship she had in college with a woman named Becky. She had come to understand this experience as "emotional dependency" and saw it as something that revealed brokenness and unhealthiness in her. She feared that her connection with Becky had ruined her for any future relationships since no one else could live up to her first love. Over the years, Jenny and Becky tried to be "just friends" many times, but each time they ended up crossing lines they had drawn and feeling like they had failed God and each other. Eventually, they cut ties.

When Jenny began to suspect that I was growing attracted to her, she confronted me. She told me she thought I was becoming emotionally dependent on her. This confrontation was awkward and embarrassing. I couldn't really deny that I had feelings for Jenny, but I didn't think I was emotionally dependent. I just knew that I cared about the relationship more than she did and that I was unhappy. She thought we could continue as roommates, but I had to get out. Depression started to roll in again. I was working at a job I hated, struggling to find friends (again!), and living in an environment that was quickly turning miserable. I couldn't talk to anyone about what was going on with Jenny.

I had a bit of a wake-up call after the 9/11 attacks. Aside from realizing that moving to the Middle East as a missionary would no longer be wise, something about seeing the Twin Towers fall made me realize that I had put my whole life on hold, waiting for a call to missions that might never come. I had been tolerating so many things in my life that I was not happy about: my job, my living situation, and my friendships. I decided to start making changes. I bought a duplex, fixed it up, started a real estate career, and looked for a church where I could make some friends that I wasn't in love with.

The first few changes happened rather quickly and left me with a renewed hope about a successful career life. Finding a church was more of a challenge. Church communities were too big, too old, or too married, and I often felt ushered into creepy singles groups. A common theme in most of these churches was a somewhat veiled hostility towards gay people. Not from everyone, of course, but from many. The churches I chose were generally silent about homosexuality from the pulpit, but there seemed to be a general consensus among the members that it was wrong to be gay. Even though I held a similar conviction that I should not act on my feelings, I was deeply disappointed and angered by how Christians targeted gay people, making them out to be the worst kind of sinners. Jokes made at the expense of gay people were common because most people held the assumption that no one among them could possibly be gay. I did not challenge their assumption.

I didn't tell anyone that I was attracted to women because, I figured, it didn't matter; I wasn't going to act on my feelings. I worried that my friends would pull away, that they would look at me differently, or that they would watch me with suspicion when I interacted with other women. I remember a conversation I'd had with Jenny around this time; she said, "I can talk about my eating disorder all day long," but she could not talk about the relationship she had had with Becky. Similarly for me, it was never easy to admit to my habit of cutting, but there was a time that I would rather have talked about that all day long than admit to being attracted to women.

After about two years of unsuccessful church shopping, I found a little Vineyard church that I called home for eight years. The Vineyard is a denomination that started up in the early seventies during the Jesus Movement, when a bunch of hippies began to challenge the formality and piousness of their parents' churches, and created a movement of peace-loving Jesus followers in blue jeans and flowers in their hair. Forty years later, most of those hippies have become Republican evangelicals. Despite many changes in the movement, it still retains a beautiful commitment to creating churches that welcome people as they are, be it poor, addicted, lonely, or downtrodden.

When I started attending the Vineyard church, I was still trying to date men, and I had not told anyone except Jenny that I was attracted to women. On my first visit, the worship pastor, with his streaked hair, ripped jeans, and rock star persona told a story from his life with such vulnerability and authenticity that I remember thinking to myself, "I will not be able to hide here." For some reason, I decided to stay anyway.

I was a little worried, at first, about the charismatic qualities of the Vineyard. I didn't see anything too strange at first. No one ran through the aisles, got "slain in the spirit," or wailed disruptively. I saw some weirdness from people who would go forward for prayer and start rocking or shaking or speaking in tongues, but it seemed to be the same few people each week and not the focus of the service. The one thing that did surprised me was the powerful prayer that occurred there. People seemed to have a supernatural ability to pray exactly what I needed to hear again and again. I was amazed at the ways God spoke through others in this community.

I grew to love this little church. People there were committed to loving each other well, to serving the poor, and to following God. This community modeled vulnerability in a way I had never seen before. People were open about their troubled pasts, their current struggles, and their moral failings. My favorite example of the openness of this church lies in my friend's story. She visited the church in the midst of the lowest low of her life. She went forward for prayer at the end of the service and said to a member of the prayer team, "I would like prayer because I might have to go to prison." The prayer team member said, "Oh, I've been there!" and proceeded to pray for her; this gave hope to my friend that she may have found a safe place to be honest about her mistakes. This friend now leads the church recovery group and tells her story of redemption to others in need of hope. This church was filled with people whose lives had been transformed by God and community.

My church was made up of rich people and poor people, young hipsters and corporate retirees, those working on their GEDs and those with PhDs. Church members were evenly split between Republican and Democrat. I loved the diversity of this church. It came with its fair share of conflict, but it still seemed both rare and valuable to know and love people who are not just like me.

The culture of vulnerability in this community did not allow me to stay in hiding for long. Secrets have a way of festering and bubbling up to the surface despite the tremendous effort it takes to keep them hidden from view. I eventually got tired of hiding and, one by one, began to share my secrets with trusted people at church. I sought help for the depression that would come in waves and color the way I saw everything around me, the self harm that would lie dormant for years and then come back with surprising intensity, and the sexual abuse that had a confusing and unexplainable power over me. The last and biggest secret was to tell was that I was attracted to women. I used this language because my faith culture didn't agree with identifying oneself as "gay" but as someone who "struggled with unwanted same-sex attractions." This is a mouthful that I was never interested in using to describe my own situation. Later on, as I tried to make light of my dilemma, I joked with one friend about having an "unwanted gayness" or about self-identifying as a "wannabe" (as in, I wannabe straight). She didn't think my joke was funny.

The first person I told at my church was my pastor, Debbie. She and I had been meeting weekly to help me overcome my need to hurt myself. As part of our work together she asked that I share an informal inventory of my life and confess any wrongs I'd done. I unloaded all of my secrets and told her about my love for women. Debbie responded kindly and suggested that we meet together and read through materials from Desert Stream Ministries on a weekly basis. Desert Stream was one of the larger ex-gay organizations affiliated with Exodus International. Debbie suggested that we work through a book titled *Pursuing Sexual Wholeness*, by Andrew Comiskey. I agreed. We met for coffee and began talking about the material. I was not expecting the emotional reaction I had. After crying repeatedly (out of my hopelessness) in a booth at Panera, I asked if we could meet somewhere more private in the future. We moved our meetings to a small room in the church so I could be less concerned about my public emotional displays.

Debbie and I met weekly, explored the roots of my same-sex attractions, and prayed for healing. The workbook encouraged building non-sexual intimacy with women and building closer relationships with men. It encouraged embracing a more traditionally feminine appearance and style of relating to others. I wasn't about to start wearing mascara and heals, but part of me thought that I should. Looking back, I wonder how I ever got to that point—in high school I had considered myself a feminist and had believed in tearing down gender stereotypes!

As Debbie and I continued to meet, I eventually stopped crying every week. We finished the twelve-week program and stopped meeting regularly. I stayed very involved in the church, taking on more leadership roles, like leading small groups, preaching at church retreats and conferences, and eventually helping launch a twelve-step recovery program.

I believe I was asked to help lead the recovery group because the pastors knew that I struggled with "unwanted same-sex attractions." Still, I never thought that working through the twelve steps would make me any less gay. By this time I wasn't really hoping to get rid of attractions to women, I was just hoping I could achieve bisexuality. I thought I might meet one man that I found attractive, reassuring myself with the thought, "It only takes one." I didn't think the recovery group could do much for me, so I focused my step work on eliminating self harm, reducing anxiety, and healing from abuse. The launch of our recovery group called for personal testimonies from each of the leaders, so I shared openly with the whole church about the abuse, self harm, and that I was attracted to women. I also shared that I believed God wanted me to marry a man someday. They gave me a standing ovation.

Thinking back on this testimony, a part of me cringes about some of what I believed. Still, I am proud that I was able to take the opportunity to share with the church how jokes and judgment of LGBTQ people were hurtful to me and to others *inside* of the church. Even while I thought I was supposed to avoid same-gender relationships, I was still frustrated with how the church treated gay people, and I was able to tell them how it affected me.

MINORITY STRESS AND MENTAL HEALTH ISSUES

Messages about the sin of homosexuality may anger and hurt queer adults, but the effects on young people are far more harmful. Adolescence is a time of insecurity for most kids, as they try to figure out who they are and how they fit among their peers. For those who feel different from their peers and unsupported by their family, it can be a miserable time. LGBTQ teens are high-risk kids. They are more likely to be bullied, abused, disowned, and homeless. They face an increased risk of mental health problems including depression, anxiety, post-traumatic stress disorder (PTSD), substance abuse, and suicide.[5] Compared with their own siblings, LGBTQ youth are more likely to seek out mental health services, engage in self harm, and attempt suicide.[6]

In his book, *Stages of Faith*, developmental psychologist James Fowler describes the spiritual interest of adolescents, saying, "The adolescent's

5. Davis et al., "Psychological Well Being of Sexual Minority Youth," 1030–41.

6. Balsam et al., "Mental Health," 471.

religious hunger is for a God who knows, accepts and confirms the self deeply."[7] As teenagers are figuring out their own identity, those with spiritual interests are looking for a God who knows them fully. Fowler states that images of God that appeal to this age group are of "a divinely personal significant other."[8] Maybe this is why we have adolescent slogans like, "Jesus is my homeboy," or "Jesus is my boyfriend." They stem from the deep need of this age group to be seen and accepted by God and others. When acceptance is hard to come by, kids tend to struggle.

In the past, the higher prevalence of mental health issues among queer people was attributed to the belief that homosexuality was a mental disorder, inherently unhealthy, and therefore associated with mental illness. Some ex-gay ministries still present this as true despite a lack of evidence and the objection of many professional health organizations. Today, it is generally accepted that the increased risk of psychiatric symptoms is related to the difficulty of being gay or lesbian in a straight man's world.

The *minority stress model* explains this phenomenon. According to this theory, members of minority groups are more likely than nonminorities to experience harassment, discrimination, exclusion, and violence. These experiences lead to increased stress as well as self-protective hypervigilance as minority people begin to expect and prepare for more painful experiences. For queer kids, negative messages are then often internalized, resulting in a shame-based self-image of being flawed, damaged, or otherwise less-than their heterosexual counterparts.[9] *Internalized homophobia* has been named one of the biggest barriers to the mental health and well-being of gay and lesbian people because of its association with guilt, depression, and feelings of worthlessness.[10]

Families and communities can play a huge role in reducing these risks.[11] When LGBTQ teens perceive their families to be unsupportive, they suffer tremendously. Those who report high levels of family rejection are nearly six times more likely to report depression, over three times more likely to use illegal drugs, and eight times more likely to have attempted suicide compared to those who report low or no family rejection.[12] Similarly,

7. Fowler, "Stages of Faith," 153.

8. Ibid., 154.

9. Meyer, "Prejudice," 674–97.

10. Wagner, "Integration," 93.

11. Ryan et al., "Family Acceptance," 205.

12. Ryan et al., "Family Rejection," 346.

LGBTQ teens who grew up in unsupportive communities were 20 percent more likely to attempt suicide than teens in supportive communities (measured by proportion of same-sex couples, proportion of Democrats, presence of in-school gay-straight alliances, and school policies that specifically protect LGBTQ students from discrimination and/or bullying).[13] This was reflected in my participants: those whose families and churches loudly expressed anti-gay messages were more likely to take on a sense of shame and engage in self-destructive behavior. Some were kicked out of homes, kicked out of churches, physically attacked, and subjected to countless lectures and conflict. They experienced depression, thoughts of suicide, shame, fear, isolation, and inner turmoil. Each person was affected in different ways, and the consequences they faced varied, but none went unscathed.

ERICKA: "INNER DEMONS"

Before meeting Ericka, I knew a little about her story: she was kicked out of her house when she came out to her mom; for years she identified as lesbian, but she is currently in a relationship with a man; and they are raising their baby together. We met for our interview at a coffee shop in a suburb of St. Paul. The church culture of her childhood was unsettling. Her mother got involved in a small Bible study that Ericka described as "radical" and "scary." They followed Levitical dietary laws and taught some unusual theology. She explained, "There was a lot of talk of demons," and the book of Revelation was "pounded into your head." These messages crossed into the bizarre as she was taught that "the next world war will be waged by aliens" and other extra-biblical ideas. These teachings gave her nightmares that lasted for years. She explained how it began:

> I grew up in the Catholic Church. It was fine until I was about eight years old when my grandmother died and my mom found a Bible study group. It wasn't the traditional Bible study; it was very radical. We attended that Bible study on Wednesday nights, yet I still went to Catholic school during the day. . . . My earliest speculation that there was a problem in what I was learning was the day I was sent to the principal's office. When I got there, my sister was there. We had been arguing with the teachers about what they were teaching us. They were telling us to pray to the Virgin Mary, and we were telling them, "No, you don't pray to anybody

---

13. Hatzenbuehler, "The Social Environment," 896.

but God." That was the first time I realized that we had a problem. It continued—my sister was able to adapt and tell the school what they wanted to hear. I wasn't able to do that. I was butting heads not just with the religion but with the school in general. It started when I was eight. When I was ten, my parents pulled me out of the school.

Getting pulled out of Catholic school was helpful for her, reducing the religious conflict, and exposing her to a (greatly appreciated) diverse student body. "[My parents] put me in an art school, which was awesome because I really got to learn more about other people. It wasn't just Catholic people. I had never gone to school with anybody of a different race or religion before, and here I was in fifth grade learning that, my friend here is Jewish, and these people are Hmong, and that's just how life is."

Despite her positive experiences in the new school, Ericka's mom remained involved in the unhealthy small group, and her home life carried a great deal of hurt and conflict. The study group her mom had joined regularly vilified gay people, and her mom joined in. Ericka recalled, "My mom started asking me if I was gay when I was sixteen. She'd ask, 'Ericka, are you a lesbian?' My response was usually a really quick, 'No, why would you think that? No.' And then occasionally [she'd] be like, 'You know, lesbians burn in hell.' It was really harsh."

This preemptive strike against her sexual orientation made it clear to Ericka that it was not safe to come out. She denied being lesbian many times before being honest with her mom.

As Ericka's identity as lesbian grew more solidified within herself, other issues began to arise. "There was a lot of self-hatred . . . during that time; a lot of inner demons that were being manifested in other ways. I struggled with an eating disorder that followed me all the way to my adulthood because there was not much I could do except overeat and then purge. I had all these emotions I didn't know what to do with. There was nobody I could turn to and talk to."

Even though Ericka's high school friends were supportive and often joked that she was "the lesbian of the group," she didn't really come to terms with her sexual orientation until after a family trip to Mexico. She remembered, "We were sitting in a terminal waiting to go, and my dad had this English to Spanish dictionary he was going through, and he was like, 'Lesbiana, that's you Ericka!' And I was like, 'Yeah.'" I asked if this was okay with her, given her mom's frequent accusations and threats of hell. She said,

"Yeah, I was okay with that. I thought, 'Dad, you're letting up,'" suggesting she saw some progress towards acceptance. She seemed secure in her relationship with her dad, saying, "He was joking; he was playful about it. That was fine. My dad has always been a good guy." Although her mom was present during this conversation, her reaction was unclear. Ericka said, "She knew; she was just so far in denial." The comment from her father stirred up some questions for Ericka about what would happen next. She said, "People go to Mexico to get drunk and float around and that wasn't me. I was taking off every day to wander in the village nearby. There was a lot of thought that went along with it, a lot of self-reflection, [like,] if I say this, this is everything that's gonna happen. But I hadn't come out to myself yet. I knew, but it just hadn't happened."

When she returned from Mexico, she started to come out to herself, and eventually to others:

> I was in beauty school at the time, and I came back and hit this ultimate low depression. The teacher came up to me and [asked], "What's going on?" . . . Two teachers were really concerned, and they [said], "Do what you need to do, we'll be here." I took a week off, and I didn't go to work and I didn't go to school. I went down to the river every day with my dog and sat there. . . . At the end of the week I cut off all my hair, got a cute cut that really identified [me]. Not that it needed to be short, but I really hated the long hair. I wanted something different. I went and got my nose pierced. And then two days later, I went to school, and my teachers could tell that something had happened. And it wasn't necessarily that I told my family because I hadn't—I told myself and I started identifying myself as a lesbian. I was open about it. I started telling my friends. I told people that were interested, but I didn't tell my family.

Ericka's self-acceptance and decision to come out to friends changed things for her. The ability to be open with her friends and to dress and look in a way that she felt was true to herself seemed to be enough for the depression to lift—and for others to notice the positive change. Ericka also did some spiritual searching during this time. Despite the strong negative religious messages she encountered about homosexuality, she still prayed for guidance and tried to develop her faith while coming to terms with her sexual orientation. "I had no idea what to believe because my whole life you're taught one thing and then all of a sudden you start feeling a different way. Then you feel like God's abandoned you. I was seventeen; I had such a hard time during that year with myself, with my sexuality. I'd go up north to camp and get away, go canoeing in the Boundary Waters for a month. That's when I would reconnect with God. I always had such a strong faith afterwards."

One trip in particular led to an experience of feeling like God had spoken to her—not in an audible voice—but in a deep sense of God's presence. This word came at a time when she desperately needed to hear it. "One day I was hiking, and I came to this awesome [place]. I was in Montana, a place very few people have ever seen. I sat down and I was like, 'Alright God, what's going on?' That was when I had this revelation; I felt God's presence with me, and I felt that—God has made all these beautiful things—I'm not a mistake! That was pretty much it. It was laid to rest then."

Later, for comfort or reassurance, Ericka often reflected on that event. When other people heaped judgment on her, she remembered that day and thought to herself, "I am not a mistake."

She continued to question the things she'd been taught and searched for truth on her own. In the searching, she experienced a depth to her faith that wasn't there before.

> The first thing I had to do was get a Bible for myself. I couldn't just keep hearing what other people had said. I found a Bible called *The Message*. I started to study it. I had hit such a low! I found the book of Job and I read that every day. [I] ultimately came to the fact that I had some serious depression/anxiety issues, and I was able to get help. . . . Because the other thing with the church that I grew up in was that it's not okay to seek medical help for depression. And so I did that hand-in-hand with the Bible. I started to study the Bible to understand it, started to apply things that I was reading to my life, and [took] on deeper spiritual practices.

Taking on these spiritual practices when she was coming out led her to a place of greater health, wellness, and spiritual growth.

Finding a healthy faith life required that she let go of her mom's condemning words and her church's authority over her life. "It really came down to—[my] faith was between God and me and nobody else. . . . That helped my faith adapt with coming out because what I was hearing from everybody else was just what I was hearing from everybody else, not what I was hearing from God." The strength of her convictions and faith eventually gave her the courage to come out to her mother. "One day my mom asked me if I was a lesbian, and I said, 'Well, what would you do if I said yes?' That was really traumatic because I got kicked out of the house. I was packing up my stuff, and my dad came and talked to me, and he said, 'I don't support this decision, I support who you are. But I think it's best for right now if you're just not here.' . . . That's pretty much how it was. I moved out and I stayed out. I moved to Texas and I didn't come home for a good year and a half."

I'm struck by the comment from her supportive father, "I think it's best for right now if you're just not here." I wonder how often it happens to those who challenge the norm, that even supportive people feel it's better for everyone that they are not around.

Ericka had little contact with her mother for the next year. She said, "We'd only talk if absolutely necessary and usually it ended in fighting. . . . She was so unreasonable and inconsolable, I couldn't have anything to do with her."

While living in Texas, Ericka got some bad news about a friend of hers. "There was a figure skating student . . . I got a call [saying] that he had jumped off the 94/494 [overpass]. It was because of his demons related with his sexuality and having faith. When you have such a raging self-hatred inside of you, there's only so much that other people can do, but I think that it's important that parents and people understand—this is serious to us! My mom thought that this was just a phase and it would stop. I can see what drove him to that point without the love and support." She remembers this friend when she hears about the deaths of other kids in the news. "I think of him when I think of people who have lost the battle. I think it's really important that tolerance is taught and that faith is taught in a way that is accepting because these people need to live—this boy was sixteen years old."

The topic of suicide came up in several interviews. Participants shared about friends or acquaintances they'd lost to suicide, or shared about a time in their own lives when they seriously considered taking their own lives. As a mental health provider, I frequently work with clients who are contemplating suicide. Depression has a way of narrowing a person's thinking so much that they can't see other options. It slowly isolates a person, changes the way they think, and limits their ability to see a future of possibilities. It is my hope that campaigns like "It Gets Better"[14] and anti-bullying movements, alongside a changing culture, will begin to reduce the tragically high suicide rates of queer teens.

14. Savage and Miller, *It Gets Better*.

There are a few people that I keep in my memory as I think of those who have been harmed most by societal and religious teachings about queer people. One young woman came to our Vineyard church drug addicted, homeless, and suicidal. Of all these things, she was most ashamed of being gay.

Coming out was a major step towards emotional health for Ericka. She wanted to hold on to her faith because, she said, "I held onto that day up in Montana where I was like, 'I am not a mistake.' I knew that people had faith out there. I'd gotten a Lavender Pages directory, and I started going to the Metropolitan Community Church—All God's Children in Minneapolis. That was what fostered my continuation of my faith. I didn't always agree with everything they said, but I needed to be there to recharge and reconnect with God. That's what fostered my faith and my sexuality."

Over time, she saw changes in her family too. "My mom had switched jobs and she started working for a nonprofit that shares the HRC [Human Rights Campaign] headquarters. And, things changed. Really, they changed." After months of no contact, Ericka made an effort to reconnect with her family. "I ended up writing them a letter touching on things that had bothered me, standing my ground, and saying, 'This is where we're at. We don't have a relationship. Do you want to have a relationship?' And that was where our turning point hit."

Now her mom is fully supportive of her—whether she chooses to date a man or a woman. Her mom even attended the wedding of her lesbian cousin. When Ericka broke up with a long-term girlfriend, her mom was disappointed and asked guiltily, "It's not because of us, is it?"

After moving back to Minnesota, Ericka reconnected with a male friend from her Boundary Waters days. "We started hanging out; we ended up developing a relationship which was different because I hadn't dated a guy since I was nineteen." She added, "He was there through everything. He was there when I came out, he was there through all my relationships. We stayed friends, so he knows every single person I've dated. We have this awesome relationship, and I think that the relationship is awesome because there's so much understanding of the past. But then I found out I was pregnant."

This pregnancy was not good news. "I was devastated. My faith really took a hike for a while. I was resentful and felt that God had left me." They decided to raise their daughter together, a decision she is now very happy about.

Ericka raved about her current life, showing disbelief that she could know such happiness and freedom. She attributed her happiness to getting help with her eating disorder, finding a supportive community, and developing her own spiritual beliefs.

> I finally got help with an eating disorder, and with that I am following a twelve-step program. My faith has been reevaluated and has been stretched apart, picked apart, reestablished. . . . My life is about turning over my will to the care of God. My spiritual practices are pretty much my Overeaters Anonymous meetings. I do a lot of studying of the AA Big Book [the basic text of Alcoholics Anonymous] and the *Twelve and Twelve* [the AA book *Twelve Steps and Twelve Traditions*], and a lot of discussion with my fellow members. I have a sponsor I speak to every morning. If I have a problem in my life, not just necessarily food related—it goes back to any problem—am I giving my will to God? Am I letting God handle this? One thing I really liked about this program is that you can be a Buddhist, a Taoist, a Jew, and we can all discuss our higher power. It doesn't matter what we believe in, but we can discuss our faith with each other. And that has fostered my growth here. One day at a time, one meal at a time. I'm renewing my faith pretty much every second of every day; it's this continuation. I love it; I'm so happy with my life right now. I know it sounds really cheesy, like, "I'm so happy!" But I have never had this freedom from self and this freedom from my mental obsession with food, and freedom from my problems.

Ericka was not attending a church at the time of the interview, showing preference for individual expression of faith and recognition of God's presence. "God is everywhere; it's not just in a church, not just in a cross. You can have spirituality in any part of your day. For me, I pray before I eat, giving things to God and taking time to recognize that God has given me this food to nourish my body with every bite. . . . I feel that God is in everything, even when I put my daughter down in her bed. That's God in my life."

At the end of the interview, Ericka reflected on her friend, the figure skating student she'd lost to suicide, and wondered if her own fate would have been much different had she been outed at a younger age. "I don't know. . . I knew I couldn't say anything because I knew what was gonna happen. I mean, look at how it was when I was nineteen. If I had been under my parents' guardianship, I would've been with Michele Bachmann's husband. (Laughs.) It just would've been bad." (Marcus Bachmann, Michele

Bachmann's husband and clinical therapist, was rumored to provide reparative therapy at his mental health clinic; something he denies.)[15]

It breaks my heart that the most damaging and prevelent messages of condemnation are coming from the Christian church. I'd like to believe that most Christians who hold a nonaffirming stance do so out of sincere commitment to their faith and belief in the trustworthiness of the Bible. Most are not motivated by hate. They've been taught that reading the Bible can lead to complete knowledge and truth on any number of moral questions. They've been taught that faith in God is demonstrated by certainty about sin. Still, most of these well-meaning Christians have no idea what these kids are going through. They don't understand, as Ericka put it, "*This is serious to us.*"

15. Kennedy, "Marcus Bachmann."

6

Impact: Violence

SOCIETAL MESSAGES OF CONDEMNATION not only have a negative impact on the mental health and developing self worth of LGBTQ people, but these messages also play a role in how others treat those who appear to be gay, creating either a safe environment or one that allows for mistreatment and abuse. Bullying and harassment in schools remain common and often carry religious messages of judgment and condemnation. Lesbian, gay, and bisexual youth are 1.7 times more likely than straight peers to experience threats of violence or physical assault. The discrepancy is higher for girls than boys. Up to 44 percent of lesbian adolescents have reported being threatened or assaulted with a weapon or otherwise physically assaulted by a peer. For straight girls, 22 percent responded affirmatively to these same questions. Additionally, LGBTQ kids are 2.7 times more likely to miss school because of fear of what could happen there.[1]

AMY: "IT WILL DESTROY AMERICA"

Amy was adopted by Jacqueline and her partner when she was nineteen years old. They met through a program that seeks to find homes for LG-BTQ kids who are homeless due to family estrangement. Amy is twenty-something, short, and butch with dark buzzed hair. She identifies herself as half Puerto Rican and half Jewish but was more heavily influenced by her Puerto Rican heritage, learning Spanish before she learned English

1. Friedman et al., "Disparities in Childhood Sexual Abuse," 1481–94.

and experiencing Catholicism that she described as "mixed with Santeria." She explained, "When the Africans came to Puerto Rico, their religion and church blended [with] the indigenous people there. Then, the Catholics had them convert, so they hid their religion in the Catholic saints. And so that's what Santeria is, it's basically voodoo." She never felt connected to her Catholic heritage and now attends a predominantly black Baptist church and considers herself conservative and affirming.

Amy was exposed to blatantly hateful teachings about gay people early on and across several different denominations, from Lutheran to Baptist to Pentecostal. She said, "Definitely in Puerto Rico with the Pentecostal church, absolutely [being gay] . . . was a disgusting thing and you are going to hell. And, a lot of the Baptist churches that I went to—same message."

These messages impacted her at a very young age since she was identifying with gay people in elementary school. She said, "I knew when I was like seven. You know, wanting to hold hands with the girls on the playground. I also knew at that age that there was something wrong about that. And no one ever really talked about gay people. I didn't know any gay people. . . . You just sort of inherently know that it's not normal—seeing everything around you and there's nothing that describes what you're feeling."

Amy's biological mother lost custody of her when she was young, and Amy was in foster care for several years. Her first adoption was into a Lutheran family when she was thirteen. They all attended church events together several times a week. "I really loved that church, until they said that gays aren't welcome, only to be fixed." Her church started to focus on anti-gay messages just as she was coming out. "At that time they were talking about breaking off from the ELCA [Evangelical Lutheran Church in America] because somebody was going to get ordained that was [gay]; it was a big topic in the church at the time. . . . And it wasn't just preaching. There were classes on it, there were videos; it was a big deal."

The teachings were not simply about adherence to a literal interpretation of the Scriptures or wanting to remain true to their traditions. "They were very clear; they were like, 'homosexuality is a sickness. . . . It's a disease in your life and it will destroy America.' I mean, that's pretty powerful: 'it will destroy America!'"

These teachings had a huge impact on Amy. "I remember being pretty devastated, because . . . I was there all the time, every Sunday, never missed. I was there on Wednesdays, I went to the retreats; anytime I could be there I was there. So, for them to say that . . . is pretty devastating." When I asked

Amy what led her to come out in this environment, she responded, "It was not a decision I made at all." She knew it wasn't safe and didn't get the chance to come out on her own terms. She added:

> Once I was outed there was no turning back. I mean, I was who I was. Then everybody in my school knew, which, there were positive moments with that, and there were a lot of negative moments with that. And, of course, I got kicked out because the lady who had adopted me found a love letter someone wrote. . . . I remember, my car was not working and I was at work, so she came to pick me up. And she was like, "Do you have something to tell me?" I had a midterm in math, and I just suck at math, and I didn't want to admit it because I'm like, "If that's not it, I'm not going to add another thing on to this." Then she threw the letter, and she punched me, and she called me all sorts of names.

Amy's recollection was so matter-of-fact, I had to go back and clarify, asking, "She hit you?" Amy continued, "She was a very violent person. But that moment. . . ." Amy paused as she gathered her words. "I felt really sick. I felt really sick about me being gay. You know? It just reinforced all those messages that I'm not living right and [I'm] going to hell."

Soon after the fight with her adoptive mom, Amy was kicked out of the house. These experiences created self-doubt that continues to this day. "They found out that I was gay, and they were like, 'You gotta go.' So from sixteen to nineteen I was homeless. That makes you [think], 'Maybe there is something wrong with me. Maybe I'm not living how I should be living.' I think that if you don't read for yourself or understand what the Bible says—that can mess you up for a long time. I'm 99 percent comfortable with my relationship and my sexuality and with God, but there's always doubt there, like, 'Am I just fooling myself?'"

Amy experienced violence at school as well. She didn't say much about the school incident in her interview, but her mom did later. Before I interviewed her mother (Jacqueline), Amy had asked if she could sit in on the interview. Jacqueline explained part of why she herself invested in anti-bullying campaigns, saying, "Amy had to drop out of high school because when she was outed as a lesbian, she was beat up."

Amy immediately corrected her: "I was not beat up!"

Jacqueline paused and said, "You were jumped."

Smiling, Amy responded, "Right. Totally different!"

"I'm supposed to say you were jumped. Sorry!"

Amy laughed and said, "They *tried* to beat me up!"

Jacqueline, smiling and nodding in remorse, said, "They tried to beat you up. Sorry. Sorry honey. I've never said that. I'm sorry."

"You're going to have to make me chocolate chip cookies."

"Alright. Sorry honey. You were jumped. God!

Jacqueline continued with her own story, explaining how she was involved in advocating for anti-bullying legislation to be passed that would protect kids from violence in schools. "I created this job at PFLAG and was working on trying to get a bill passed through the legislature. I've worked with rainbow families, I mean, years and years of stuff, and what has it resulted in? Nothing concrete. Nothing. . . . The law that we almost got passed—Pawlenty vetoed [referring to the governor of Minnesota at the time]."

Amy piped in, "He's a douche bag."

Jacqueline explained, "He was running for president and he couldn't have that. He couldn't be seen as being supportive of beat-up gay kids." Then she paused and said to Amy, "Some of them *were* beat up. You might not have been, but some of them were!"

Coming out is an act of courage and self-acceptance as people stand against what is expected of them, face the judgment of others, and proclaim what they know to be true of themselves. Being outed, on the other hand, takes away a person's power to make their own decisions, to define themselves on their own terms, and subjects them to the criticism, rejection, violence, or other consequences they may have feared. While coming out is often empowering, being outed is the opposite and can have tragic results. To use a very public example, Rutgers student, Tyler Clementi, was outed by his roommate, who used a hidden camera to record Tyler kissing another man in his dorm room. This roommate then spread the video around campus, encouraging others to watch. Within days Tyler ended his life by jumping off the George Washington Bridge.[2]

After getting kicked out of her home and knowing she wasn't welcome in her Lutheran church, Amy gave up on her faith for a while. Her experiences of rejection and teachings of this church led her to wonder if she was destined for hell.

> When I found out that I was not accepted in the Lutheran Church—the church that I thought I would go to forever . . . I

2. Foderaro, "Private Moment," A1.

was like, 'If I'm going to hell I'm going to be the best at being bad. (Laughing.) I'm gonna do as much crap as I can do on my way.' I think a lot of gay people fall away from the church and are lost because they've been told they're going to hell. So what's the point in trying to live right? . . . So, for a while I was just the baddest. You know I did that well!"

Let it be known that telling people they are going to hell does not make them want to change for the better.

About a year after getting kicked out of her home and leaving her church, Amy started attending a Baptist church. I wondered what led her to a conservative Baptist church after all she had been through already. She said, "I was having a crisis in my life at the time. I was homeless. Through a friend, I had been going to this church that was very Bible-based." She was drawn to churches with a strong emphasis on the Bible. "When I was learning to read, one of the first of books was the children's Bible. So you get all the stories down, and then you start reading the adult versions of that, and I think it just fit. It was more in line with what I internally believed."

Early on, she met with the pastor and was open about her orientation. Her pastor's response was, "You need to be celibate." Amy replied, "Okay, I can do that," and she followed her commitment. When a friend of hers at church gave her a small kiss, the pastor witnessed it and got angry. Amy tried to explain, "It was just a friend thing; it was nothing. I had really been sticking to it." The pastor "wasn't hearing any of it." He said to her, "No. You can't . . . we don't do that and you can't come back here."

After being asked to leave, she gave up on the church again for several years. "I did try for many years, unsuccessfully, to be straight. Just to try to live right—according to what they were preaching. But, you know, it didn't work out." She laughed and added, "Thank God!" According to Amy, try-ing to be straight involved: "Abstinence. And then trying to be with men. Abstinence is just depressing; to be celibate, I don't think that that's natural. And then being with men—again—depressing. I mean, they're good for friends, or pets, but not for partners."

Amy explained the futility of her experiences, saying, "When I was trying to be straight, I really tried, and then . . . at a certain point I'm just like, 'I can't do this!'"

When Amy was nineteen, she was adopted by Jacqueline, and the two of them started attending Jacqueline's Catholic church together and eventually got confirmed together. Amy described her reasons for maintaining her faith life despite so many negative experiences:

> It was something that's always there. It's sort of like breathing—
> even though I had a lot of pain around God and my faith. I actually
> questioned whether He even existed, and that was of late. I had a
> lot of pain in my life in general, so to add the gay thing on top of
> that was the last straw. But, the relationship I used to have with
> God . . . I felt pretty whole. In my young adult years, running wild
> and not having a care in the world feels pretty empty. I've been
> filling a hole with crap, and none of that was working. I think the
> only thing that worked was my faith. And I'm not totally there yet.
> I have days where I feel like I'm on the right track with God, and
> then there are days when I'm just like, just "I'll talk to you later."
> (Laughs.)

Amy was still able to look to God for a sense of wholeness despite her painful experiences.

Amy had to go through a process of adopting affirming Christian beliefs. Essential to her process of finding an affirming faith was gaining understanding about what the Bible really says and how it should be interpreted. "I think you have to understand what it's really talking about because if you just read it from an eight-year-old['s] perspective then you're not going to understand. And that's important for me because I do believe in it literally, and I would like to live according to what's right." She added, "Understanding the whole gay piece—the few times it's mentioned in the Bible and understanding that I wasn't going to hell" was the most important thing she gained from a deeper understanding of the Bible.

Amy also worked on separating the teachings of certain people from what she knew to be true about God. She doesn't mince words when talking about the human condition. "Humans can be extremely evil, but that's their free will. They chose that path, and they're choosing to do harm to others. That doesn't have anything to do with God. That has to do with us as human beings. I guess I knew that at a young age, that God isn't this vengeful person that's gonna get back at you because you didn't go to confession." I asked about her inherent sense that God was good. She explained, "God [is] good and people are bad . . . is basically it."

Amy's faith reveals how spiritual beliefs can create resiliency, helping people make sense of pain and suffering. Separating God from the evil in the world helped her to maintain faith after surviving abuse, the foster care system, a failed adoption, homelessness, and rejection from her church.

She has now has a stable home and a family, and she has found a faith community that she enjoys. It is a "Bible-based" black Baptist church. She believes that this church is moving towards full inclusion with the help of the pastor, but the community isn't quite there yet. She still goes to church in a suit and tie and feels comfortable being herself there.

7

Impact: Broken Relationships

ALL OF THE WOMEN I interviewed experienced some conflict with others, whether it was within families, churches, or friendships. Often, this conflict led to complete loss of relationships that were once very important. Conservative Christians leaders have often advised their followers to respond to LGBTQ people by taking a firm stand on moral issues and making their disapproval known. While some people might graciously add, "But God still loves you," this approach is not loving and has alienated queer people from Christian churches, friends, and families. Renae's story highlights the pain involved in the loss of relationships. She lost friends from her church when she came out, but the bigger loss was the "excommunication" by her mother that lasted several years and the ongoing conflict and judgment she faces.

RENAE: "DAY-TO-DAY I WAS LIVING A LIE"

I met Renae through mutual friends from my old church. She is twenty-nine, mixed race, about five foot four, and has light brown skin and curly black hair. She finds herself challenging others' preconceived ideas about what a lesbian might look like, as she is more feminine, wearing long hair, funky earrings, makeup, and scarves. I knew her before coming out myself, and I felt some tension as we both expected judgment from the other. After I came out, we were able to speak much more freely with one another, which was a blessing to me and essential to our interview. In her story of coming out, Renae was deeply motivated by personal integrity—living out of her true self and no longer keeping secrets in self-protection. She faced rejection and judgment in order to obtain authenticity in relationships with others, and with authenticity came self-respect.

At the time of her interview, Renae was busy working on a doctoral degree and settling into a new home with her partner. She described her early faith life, saying:

> The first church that I have fond memories of was 95 percent African American and other people of color. And I think that my mom [who is white] felt ostracized there and felt challenges with being a single mother after her husband, who was African American, died. From there we went on to some Assemblies of God churches, some nondenominational churches, [and] some churches that identified as Baptist. Those early memories are really diverse in terms of the types of environments we went to. [I] definitely had a breadth of experience.

Despite the wide variety of cultures in the churches she attended, they all taught that homosexuality was a sin. She describe her church involvement as one of the most formative aspects of her upbringing: "The kind of community that I most closely identified with—at a very early age, all the way until high school—was the church community." Her family was clearly dedicated to church life. "The amount of time that we spent there . . . Sundays, Sunday school, and usually a Sunday night service; Wednesdays were youth groups, my mom had a cell group, and on the weekends there was always something for youth. Then, there you go, you spend three to four nights a week with that faith-based community." She described the impact these communities had on her, saying, "It was a huge influence in that the majority of my relationships were through the church, be it peers, mentors, or people that we spent time with playing. My first jobs were all related to those relationships that were built in the church, so I think it was one of those primary things that influenced a lot of what I did."

Renae seemed to appreciate these connections but also wished she'd been exposed to other worldviews, especially as she was coming out. She described a slow process of growing aware of her sexual preference.

> I don't think it's something I can pinpoint. I knew when I was in middle school. Maybe sometime between fifth and seventh grade. I'd say that I had a depth of feeling for girls that other girls that I was friends with didn't have. I just thought I was a really loyal

friend—and perhaps I was, but I think that it didn't start to manifest itself until I was sixteen and older. Then my peer group had started to experiment sexually, and I had no desire. And I've had boyfriends, but I never felt like I was attracted to them. I found similarities and things that we could connect about—usually music or sports—but when it came to like, wanting to kiss, I'd hear my friends talk about it, and I couldn't connect to how they were feeling.

Despite growing awareness of her orientation as lesbian, she didn't act on these feelings for several years. She explained part of the reason for her hesitancy. "I grew up in an extremely strict household. My brother found ways to rebel, and I turned into a super disciplined, strict child. . . . It wasn't until I was a senior in college, and I was like, 'You know what? I can have fun!' . . . It wasn't until I relaxed and got outside of some of those relationships that I felt constricted by that I realized, 'My gosh, I could actually have a relationship, and this is what it could actually look like!'"

She seemed excited about the prospect of finding a relationship with a woman. She also knew that coming out would not be easy. It took some time for Renae to get to such a place of self-acceptance and letting go of old messages she'd been taught.

I knew from a young age that I was different, and I grew up in churches that definitely do not condone homosexuality to a point where some of the churches and some of the people that I loved and cared for would go out of their way to be bigots and propagate that bigotry using religion, which is really hard. . . . I knew that there was something about me that wasn't right, and for a long time I internalized. I don't know if it was shame or confusion. It might've been all of the above. Some of it was based on religion, but some of it was based on [how] I felt like day-to-day I was living a lie. I couldn't be honest with people about how I was feeling.

Renae started coming out to her closest friends and professors who she knew would respond with support and acceptance. For her, coming out was "a way to live out that authenticity." She explained: "With so many of my other relationships, I couldn't be fully myself, and I couldn't share these aspects about my life." She built up a support network and sought out others who were farther down the path, able to give her hope for an integrated spiritual life. "It's been a process over the last two decades of really wondering if how I was feeling or thinking was sinful and wrong, to now, knowing that who I am and who I choose to be intimate with is not going to send me to hell. I really credit the relationships with people who, more than anything, were mentors." Meeting other affirming people of faith was "the defining thing" for Renae. "I didn't feel affirmed until I found myself in communities where there were other people like me."

After building up a support network, Renae began a slow process of coming out to others, which, she said with a laugh, "continues to this day." When old friends from church learned about Renae coming out, these friends stopped returning her texts and phone calls. Renae said, "I got the hint." The most painful loss was her relationship with her mother.

Renae was especially articulate in describing the pain of parental rejection. She longed to come out to her mother despite knowing that it wouldn't go well. Describing her mother, Renae said, "She believes in absolutes; there is right and wrong and black and white, and it's hard for her to see anything in between." In addition, "She would make jokes about people who are homosexual in my presence and in my brother's presence, not knowing that I was a lesbian." This dynamic and their church culture made it quite difficult for Renae to be open with her mom. "I struggled for more than three years [with] how to come out to my mother. There were times where I mustered the strength, and I had a script in my head of what I could say, and I just couldn't do it. I think the fear and anxiety really got to me. Then I thought I could do it in a letter. One day I tried to start it seventeen different times, and I just couldn't."

Eventually, her mom did find out. Renee described that day, saying, "It's hard for me to remember because it's all sort of blurry and painful." After graduation from college, Renae rented a room in a house shared by two other lesbian women. When her mom met her new roommates, it apparently dawned on her that her daughter could be lesbian as well. She immediately reacted with contempt and left in the middle of their meal. Renae tried to reach out to her mom:

> I called her up. I kept calling and calling and calling. It took a few days before she'd answer my call, and then [she asked], "Do you have something you need to tell me?" Then there was the conversation that didn't last that long—I came out to her. Then I didn't hear from her for a few weeks, so I wrote a letter, and I didn't hear from her for a very long time. Then there was an email that basically said, "I can forgive you if you choose to acknowledge that this is a sin and seek forgiveness and healing." And I called her and left a message [saying] that that was not possible.

Renae stood her ground as she tried to maintain a relationship with her mother. "I ended up going to her house knowing that she would likely not welcome me in—which she didn't—but we had a conversation on her doorstep. For her, it came down to her faith, that she didn't raise a daughter who was a lesbian. She said some hurtful things, and after that there was an excommunication of a couple years."

Renae's choice of the words reveals the position of spiritual authority her mother had in her life, holding the power to cast her out of fellowship. Renae continued to reach out to her mom despite hurtful words being said. After years of little to no contact, they've spent the last few years building their relationship to a place where they can have civil dialogue with one another and stay involved in each other's lives. The relationship is clearly tense, but progress has been made.

> I am not a fighter, but she is very confrontational. And for being a tiny little thing physically, she is able to really verbally intimidate people. It's hard because I'm not going to out-yell her. I'm not going to out-Scripture her. I really tried that and it didn't work. So really it's about meeting her where she's at and let[ting] her know, "This is what I need from you; I would like a relationship. I want to integrate all of who I am into my relationship with you and not feel like I'm lying or hiding or feeling ashamed about anything." So I agreed to be who I am, and proud of it, and I think she agreed to continue a relationship. . . . I don't think she'll ever be a member of PFLAG, and I think that's okay. I've seen a change in her since I started dating my current partner. Now, she will let [my partner] into her home. I think that that is huge.

Renae tries to be generous with her mother and to give her credit for small progress in order to maintain a relationship today. "I have to understand that for over twenty years, she knew me as one way and to try and think of me as another way that betrayed her principles and her beliefs would be difficult. So, fast forward to current day; we have a relationship, but it's very surface. I refer to it as intimate strangers. We know just enough about each other, and then we know when to stop because we will enter into territory that we just know we don't agree on."

Renae is able to see that sometimes little changes are a pretty big deal. She still holds out hope that her mom could continue to grow and that their relationship could improve: "Who knows, I think that it could change should I decide to have children. I saw an entirely different side of her when she was a grandmother with my nephew. She has a hard exterior, and I think it's very difficult to crack. And it was really beautiful to see her with my nephew. I think that she's able to love him in ways that she wasn't able to do with my brother and I."

Renae and her partner have recently started looking for a faith community that they could enjoy together. After her separation from the church, Renae started to recognize the pieces that she missed.

> Something that I will always want and need are communities of people that I feel a part [of]—be it faith-based community, or professional collaborative community, or just a community of friends. I spent time thinking about it; I prayed about it, I talked with other people about it. Doing all those things, I've realized that I really do want to belong to a community of believers who share the same beliefs and who live affirming lives. I think that it's something I need, just for the edification of making me grow. My growth has been hugely impacted by religion, by spirituality; until the age of twenty-five I was in a faith-based community. Now that I'm twenty-nine it's been really interesting to see things I've missed, the things that I know that I've decided, "Yes, this is what I want."

They have not yet found the right community, but Renae still finds herself in a place of contentment about her faith. "I think my faith is the healthiest it's ever been because I am able to be honest with myself, honest with others. I sought out relationships that affirm me in healthy ways and challenge me to grow." She added that losing people she cared about because of their judgment of her was painful. "So, it was easy for me to shut down and be resentful. I've worked through a lot of stuff, and I can't say that all the bitterness is gone, but in terms of my faith, and being alive, and how I act, and the activities I choose to invest my time in, I'm happy about it. I'm at a place where I reconciled being a Christian and having a faith with being a lesbian and knowing that they are not mutually exclusive, but they're just parts of my identity."

Reconciliation of these parts of her identity has allowed Renae to become more of an advocate. Initially she came out to find support. Now, she comes out to others in order to "dispel any myths." She has been involved in diversity groups and faith groups that promote safe communities for LGBTQ people and seemed surprised by courage she has found within herself as well as the health that has come from authentic living

MAUREEN: IN-LAWS IN CHRIST

Maureen is a young, socially conscious attorney who was referred to me by Anita. They both had similar stories of hiding a significant relationship from their families for several years. Bright, driven, and passionate, Maureen was outraged by the brand of Christianity that she encountered after moving to Minnesota. She grew up in California, going to catechism with her siblings and Sunday mass with her mom. She enjoyed church but added a small disclaimer, "The only thing I didn't enjoy is that we went to eight o'clock mass every Sunday." Despite their consistent attendance, Maureen said, "Being Catholic didn't necessarily define our family because my father wouldn't go to church, my sisters didn't go to church. It was just me and my mom."

At the time of the interview, Maureen and her wife, Sara, had been together for seven years, married for three. Maureen and Sara (who grew up in a small town in Minnesota where she attended an evangelical church) have made an effort to bring the spiritual dimension into their marriage, insisting they be married in a church despite Sara's family's objections, and maintaining personal spiritual practices of prayer and Bible reading. In addition to her full-time job, Maureen volunteers as an advocate in the courts for children who have been abused or neglected or are involved in custody disputes.

As Maureen described her upbringing, church was one place where she could get her mother all to herself. "I'm the youngest of five children; I was the only one [who] would go to church with my mom, so it was our Sunday tradition. . . . Every single Sunday we'd sit in the same section. I enjoyed it because you got to see the same people, you said hello, you gave hugs. And after church every Sunday they had a pancake breakfast, so you'd go and have breakfast with everybody in the congregation."

When I asked if she grew up with negative messages about homosexuality, she said, "No, I didn't. It honestly was not talked about when I was young. It wasn't a bad thing or a good thing, it just didn't exist almost." It never even occurred to her that she could be lesbian until she was away at college, when, she said, "it dawned on me that there were other possibilities." After she "explored some things," she realized, "Oh, this makes sense!"

Growing up in the church, Maureen knew that her religion did not approve of homosexuality, but she wasn't influenced by their position. Her relationships never went against her own belief system. "Not my beliefs, my personal beliefs, but the beliefs of the Catholic religion. . . . I didn't feel wrong about it and think that I was going against God's word, or I was sinning. But I knew that it was wrong in the eyes of the Catholic Church, and I knew that my mother especially thought it was wrong and thought it was a sin." Maureen kept her first relationship with a woman a secret from her family for several years. After the breakup, she felt a growing internal pressure to reach out to them for support. When I asked what led her to come out, she replied: "I finally felt that I wasn't gonna *not* be gay. When I broke up with my girlfriend in college I was alone; my dad had just passed away, and I was lost. I had nobody to turn to. Because, my friends . . . they can only give you so much. I think it had a lot to do with my dad passing away. It was like, they don't know me. . . my family doesn't know me. This huge part of me I was hiding from them, and I finally just decided, I can't handle it anymore all by myself."

She made phone calls to each of her four siblings and her mother all in one night. Maureen was surprised when her sisters told her, "We've known since you were born!" Maureen asked them, "Why didn't you tell me? Because I didn't!" She laughed as she added, "It could have saved me a lot of time!" Apparently her family knew her a little better than she thought.

Maureen's family was largely supportive when she came out, especially after some time to adjust to the news. "I got some backlash from my mom, but not too much. My sisters have always been on my side. They've never said anything negative to me because they're my older sisters and, according to them, they already knew, so they had a long time to get used to it. But my mom gave me the [most] hassle."

Maureen's arguments with her mom make me smile because, in her words, "everything is kind of like a grain of salt when we talk because we're Italians and we argue all the time." They make big threats and quickly make up. When Maureen came out to her mom, she recalled, "She acted like she didn't understand." Maureen argued, "Mom, you know what I'm talking about!" After some explanation:

> She was like, "Well, you know that I think it's a sin, and this isn't what you're supposed to do. But you're my daughter and I love you." She said it a lot more irrational[ly], but [that's] the kind of relationship I have with my family. We're very open and blunt with each other. I told her, "You know what mom? I don't care if you think it's wrong, and I don't care if you think God thinks that it's a sin. I think it's right, so this is me. If you can't be okay with it, then I don't want you to be a part of my life." And she's like, "Oh, don't act like that."

Apparently, her mom tried to start an argument a few other times, but Maureen said, "I put her in her place right away," and told her, "just keep your thoughts to yourself if they're gonna hurt me." Now, years later, Maureen's mom calls Sara her daughter and is very supportive.

Maureen's bigger challenge was dealing with the "brutal" Minnesota family she married into. When her partner, Sara, came out to her family about their relationship, Maureen and Sara had many long and drawn out arguments with Sara's family.

> When Sara and I first decided to get married, we told her parents, and we had this huge conversation about the Bible, and how it's wrong, and Leviticus—I'm serious. We sat down and they talked about the Bible. I said to them, "You know what? You live your life on the Bible, and that's fine if that makes you happy and if you are enjoying your life. But I don't live my life on the Bible; I live my life on my own values. The Bible is just a guide to me to do the right things." You can imagine how that blew up in my face. They started quoting Scripture, and I started quoting Scripture back to them. Because you're not supposed to use the Bible as a sword, but I have to. I have to defend myself. They would quote Leviticus, and then I would say, . . . "You know, the Bible also says, 'Don't judge and you won't be judged. Forgive and you will be forgiven.' You don't judge! It's not your place!" And I've had a lot of hard talks with her parents, and then her aunt, and letters, and her grandparents with letters.

I had to ask about all these letters she referenced. "Her aunt sent us two pages, single spaced, typed letter on how the devil has our soul and a bunch of outrageous religious beliefs. I'm like, 'Are you kidding me right now?' It made me angry."

It didn't stop with the letters. After getting engaged, Maureen and Sara were invited to meet with a couple of Sara's aunts for dinner, which Maureen admitted was "probably not a good idea." She remembered, "They were telling us, 'Why can't you just go elope? Why do you have to do a religious ceremony?'" Maureen explained, "We did this very spiritual ceremony with [Sara's] pastor and God was in it. It was us; I cannot hide who I am. It was us, and God was in it, and Scripture was in it. We picked [the verses] out. So, her aunts were saying, 'This is wrong for you to have a religious ceremony because marriage in religion is for a man and a woman.'"

Maureen argued at length with these aunts about biblical passages and her own sense of right and wrong. She told them, "I have certain beliefs and

I have certain morals that I follow in my life, and I am not breaking any of those." Her words fell on deaf ears. "Of course they didn't listen to a word I said because they're irrational, and when you speak to people who are irrational about their religious beliefs they don't listen to anything you have to say. She was like, 'It's just so wrong! It's so wrong!'"

Maureen remembered another incident of crossing this aunt when she visited Sara's hometown church on Easter Sunday. At this point, church had become difficult for Maureen to attend for other reasons. "I associated church with my dad's death. So after my dad died, every single time I went to church I bawled—every single time." She added, "I can contain myself a little bit, but it's very emotional for me. And then on top of [that], being gay, and the people say things, and it's just like, 'really? Can you just leave me alone?'"

Recalling this Easter with Sara's family, Maureen said, "Easter is my favorite holiday, so I was all happy." At this congregation, there was a time during the service when members could stand up and say a prayer out loud. Maureen recalled, "Of course her aunt grabs the mic." To the whole community, Sara's aunt prayed, "I pray for those in this room who are lost and need to find God's way." Maureen was angry. "I knew she was talking to us. I knew she was talking to us, and I just started bawling. It was already emotional to be in church anyway, and then I was just like, 'Oh my God I can't handle this.' So I went to the bathroom and I was just crying."

Sara's mom tried to reach out to Maureen, saying, "Never mind her she's a kooky aunt; no one really likes her." They took a walk outside in their dresses despite the cold Minnesota spring, and the conversation continued:

> Her mom was saying, "You're gonna have to give us time to get used to it. We love you, we love our daughter. No, we don't think you should be in intimate relationship; we think marriage is for a man and a woman." And when somebody says that to me I just want to deck them. Can you not say that? I mean, what is the point of saying that? To make you feel better? Because I already know that's how you feel. But I was just like, "Whatever." I just rolled my eyes at that. She was like, "You're just gonna have to give us a chance, and some people will never accept it and never agree with you. And unfortunately her aunt is one of them."

Sara's mom was right in that they needed time to adjust and that Sara's aunt would probably never change. Maureen saw progress with the rest of the family, though.

> I am lucky that Sara's mom and dad are on board with us now. They are completely fine with it. They love us, and I have a great relationship with her parents. They love me like their own child, but that took three years. We're finally at that place right now where we say "I love you" to each other. Little things like when we're talking on the phone, her mom will call me and be like, "Blah blah blah blah," and I'll say, "Whatever." And she'll be like, "Okay, I love you, bye." We're finally to that point. It took a lot of hard work and a lot of holding back on my end. (Laughing.)

Maureen apparently had to bite her tongue quite a bit. It's clear from her story that she also did her fair share of speaking her mind. She seems very grateful for the relationship she does have with her in-laws and for the progress they've made.

Despite the progress they've seen, Maureen is still affected by all that occurred between family members. She says, "It's [caused me to] questioned my faith a lot. . . . I don't do certain things because of [Sara's] family." She gave an example:

> Just little things; when someone sneezes, [you] say, "Bless you." I don't do that anymore. I question myself. If I say "Bless you" to them, what does it mean to them? What if they don't believe in God? What if they don't believe in the same things? I'm blessing them and it might offend them, and all these things are going through my head. So every time somebody sneezes, I don't do anything because I'm like (laughing), I don't know what's correct and what's not. People have questioned me, and I've questioned them so much, who knows? So, I don't ever talk about religion or ever incorporate it in my daily life with friends or strangers. Unless I know they think the exact same way as me, and nobody thinks the exact same way as me.

We laughed at this example, but it shows how much this conflict has impacted her ability to speak freely. Now she worries that her kind word will be perceived as offensive.

Maureen and Sara seem very grateful for their current faith, the religious ceremony they were able to have for their wedding, and the growth they've seen in many family relationships. They have not yet found a faith community to suit their needs, but they were keeping up some spiritual practices with each other. Maureen spoke of bringing prayer and Bible reading into their daily lives and encouraging each other with reminders like, "God loves you and I do, too." Maureen explained the importance of her faith to her now:

> I live my life around certain things like the serenity prayer. We have that in our bathroom. I like to have that kind of joy and faith and hope in my life. It makes me feel good about myself and makes me a better person. And really, if I don't believe in something, I will be a miserable person because there's so many horrible things in this world and there's so many horrible people and actions and natural disasters. If I don't have faith, something to hope for, or something to believe in, I will be an angry, miserable, depressed person. It helps me get through the hard times.

Maureen learned to see God as a constant comfort. She felt like God would say to her, "If you don't think anybody in this world cares about you, at least I do. If you don't think anybody in this world loves you, at least I do." She went on to describe the kind of love that she believes God offers, saying, "It's constant. It's unconditional love that's always going to be there; that caring is always gonna be on your side." Her words strike me as the words of someone who has experienced God's love and has been changed by it.

MY STORY: CONFLICT, LOSS, AND MENTAL HEALTH CRISES

Renae was devastated by rejection by her mom and the loss of the relationship they once had. Maureen felt forever changed by conflict with her in-laws. Losing friends and family in the coming out process remains a sad reality for many in conservative and moderate Christian environments. My story is a little backwards. I accepted my church's teachings regarding celibacy for LGBTQ people, and this caused some atypical problems between me and my parents. They were telling me to come out and accept my lesbian self while I objected, "No, it's wrong!" Funny, but true. Meanwhile, conflict with friends led me to reconsider my firmly held beliefs.

In the years to follow my move into my own home, my friendship with Jenny dwindled. Her depression worsened, which led her to isolate from people she cared about. I didn't fully understand what was going on with her; it just seemed like she didn't want to spend time with me. I felt hurt and eventually let our friendship die off. She made no attempt to keep in contact. After about a year of no contact with Jenny, I learned that Becky had moved to town. This is the same Becky who had been Jenny's secret girlfriend and greatest weakness.

It was an incredibly random coincidence. I'd been renting out a room in my house to a friend from church. This roommate went out one night in order to meet a friend of a friend who was new to Minneapolis and didn't know anyone in town. An out-of-town friend had arranged their meeting in the hopes that my roommate could help this newcomer get to know some local people. While they were at dinner, I got a text asking if I knew of a Becky from college. I certainly did. Becky was not only Jenny's former love, but she had captured my attention the first time I saw her. She sang "O Happy Day" at one of our campus meetings, and I was captivated. Here she was in Minneapolis where she knew no one except me, my roommate, and Jenny—with whom she was not speaking.

I sat stunned for a while. I wanted to call her. I questioned my motives. She seemed like a dangerous choice for a friend. Still, I felt for her. I knew she held her secrets tight, and I wanted her to know that communities exist where she could be open and not have to hide. My church had provided such an environment for me, and I wanted to share my people with her. I was already feeling a clear calling to LGBTQ people, so I invited her into my life. She came in like a tornado.

We were incredibly close and we drove each other crazy. She wanted to know everything about me and demanded that I not fall in love with her. I thought that keeping strong boundaries with her would keep our friendship safe—that I could avoid falling for her if I kept a certain emotional distance. She encouraged me to let down my guard. I thought that so many of her friends had fallen in love with her because she had poor boundaries, so I wasn't about to let my walls down.

Becky stormed through my social sphere as well, throwing my peaceful friendships into conflict. She made enemies with two of my closest friends and became very close with one of my friends, Elaine. Elaine was a few years older than I and had been married (to a man) for over ten years. For a while the three of us were the best of friends, but even then it involved a lot of conflict. Becky was high energy, feisty, fun, creative, and a bit of a bulldog. She was intense about everything she did. She could sing better than anyone I'd ever met and carried both confidence and a very hidden but intense sense of shame.

Elaine was a bit more reserved, with a sarcastic, even cynical, sense of humor. She was intensely devoted to her friends, going out of her way to be helpful or to demonstrate care. She was the first to jump up and help out with anything, she always brought extra beer, and she sent random funny cards expressing encouragement. She asked great questions and made a point to listen well. Despite all of these wonderful qualities, she was rarely able to open up to others. I was no exception; she encouraged me to share all that was going on in my life but wasn't able to share about her own.

I felt incredibly lucky to have made such wonderful friends. Elaine and Becky both engaged in friendships with a level of intimacy that I had never experienced before, and I loved them. Knowing them has changed me forever.

Conflict with my family was fairly intense at this time. It started back when I was living with Jenny. I was starting to feel bombarded by issues connected to homosexuality: gay rights issues were at the front of the news on a daily basis; Rev. Gene Robinson became the first openly gay bishop of the Episcopal Church; and George W. Bush was backing the Federal Marriage Amendment limiting marriage to heterosexual couples. Then, an event changed my family forever: my little brother came out. It had never occurred to me that David might be gay. My parents attended one PFLAG meeting and quickly became advocates. Soon they were marching in the Pride parade and telling their story of accepting their gay son to anyone who would listen.

Regretfully, I thought it was my responsibility to tell my brother where I stood on "the issue." I told him that I loved him no matter what, and that I thought it was wrong to pursue same-sex relationships. David, being a very gracious brother, accepted me anyway. I never brought it up again, and we managed to maintain a positive relationship of mutual respect and difference of opinion.

Getting along with my parents was another story. They swung from Catholic, Republican, Pro-Life conservatives to flaming liberals in no time. Suddenly, it seemed like everything they did was gay! My mom was president of the Minnesota chapter of PFLAG, and my dad was involved in Catholic gay advocacy groups. They became such outspoken advocates that they were asked to stop talking about anything related to homosexuality at their Catholic church. My mom was devastated. She stopped attending church for the first time in her entire life. She and my dad grew angry at Christians who couldn't change their minds as quickly as they did. They threw around terms like "hateful" and "ignorant" to describe people who held opposing views. This angered me. I was in no way ignorant about homosexuality; they had no idea how much thought, prayer, and reading I'd already put into my beliefs. I'd made it clear that I loved my brother and I was treating him well. Still, I felt judged. Our relationship grew very strained. I had not yet told them I was lesbian, but they were on to me.

One Sunday afternoon I joined my parents to watch a Vikings game at their house. Completely out of the blue, my mom asked, "Rachel, are you gay?" My initial response was anger. She knew how my religious beliefs would not allow me to act on those feelings, even if I did have them. Letting the uncomfortable silence linger, I stared her down for a moment. Eventually, I admitted that I was generally attracted to women, but that I could never act on those feelings because they went against my religious beliefs.

The mix of pity and condescension I felt from my parents for the following year was infuriating. They continued to use words like "bigoted," "hateful," and "ignorant" to describe people who had religious beliefs that opposed homosexuality. They seemed to suggest that I was just uninformed, as if they knew more than I did about what it's like to be gay.

Now, I can see that they were concerned. They picked up on the energy between me and Becky and wondered if I was hiding a sexual relationship from them. They sensed my unhappiness and wanted to help. They believed that coming out and dropping my religious beliefs would be what was best for me. They may have been right, but I couldn't just drop my beliefs. I needed to find my own way.

Shortly after Becky moved into town and after the twelve-step recovery group (that I was leading at my church) began, my real estate career began its downward spiral. The market shifted, the phone stopped ringing, and both my new townhouse and duplex plummeted in value. Transactions that were once fairly simple would fall apart as buyers got cold feet, lenders cracked down on requirements, appraisers got stricter, and homes that were being sold on contingency never made it to closing. I was in trouble. My credit cards were maxed out, and I couldn't find another job that would cover the mortgage. I didn't have a backup career plan, and I didn't know what to do. It was soon apparent that I would have to go through bankruptcy and foreclosure, in addition to finding a new career.

The twelve-step group turned out to be a much needed place for me to lay down the image of success (that realtors are encouraged to keep up) and be honest about my depression, career failure, and loss of home. I was able to be honest with people about current struggles like I never had been before. I no longer had any secrets, and the group still cared for me. I received love and support from people who were worse off than I was. They developed in me a love for people who struggle, and I counted myself one of them. It soon became harder to connect with the overly religious Christians who hid their problems and seemed to have their lives together. Taking part in this group prompted me to go back to school for social work. I discovered that I loved working with the down and out. My volunteer work seemed to be a better fit for me than any job I'd ever had. The group was a beautiful thing.

My group of friends also went out of their way to show support to me during this time. I felt, for the first time in my life, that I was surrounded by wonderful people and that I wasn't hurting for friends. Elaine and Becky were two of the most wonderful friends I'd ever known. But our little group of three started to break apart. The ongoing conflict with Becky was tiresome, and the intensity of our friendship didn't seem healthy to me. I thought Becky was blind to how her style of relating to her friends encouraged them to fall in love with her. She didn't see a backrub, a hand on the thigh, or sharing the most intimate details of our lives as romantic. We both thought the problem in our friendship was with the other person.

As conflict grew in my friendships with Becky and Elaine, time spent with them became uncomfortable. I was beginning to feel edged out. They would sneak away from the crowd at parties to spend time alone together and whisper to each other in front of me. Hanging out with either one of them was great, but spending time with both of them together was strangely awkward. Eventually, any time I spent with Becky, she would vent about how Elaine's marriage was inadequate and her husband didn't support her. They were falling in love—it seemed clear to everyone except Becky, Elaine, and Elaine's husband. I tried many times to ask Elaine about her marriage since she spent so little time with her husband. She always claimed that the marriage was wonderful—that they may spend a lot of time apart, but their marriage was strong.

My conflict with Becky grew more intense than I could tolerate, and we decided to take a break, which turned into a permanent severing of ties. Elaine stopped spending time with me, too. She gave no explanation and pulled away from nearly all of her other friendships. Within months she left her husband and moved in with Becky. Becky and Elaine both claimed their relationship was not romantic, despite how it seemed to others. They both pulled away from friends they'd known for years and seemed to disappear from their social circles.

The dynamics of this drama resulted in me losing Becky, Elaine, and most of my other closest friends as our group fell apart. I was devastated. I began to look at what I could have done differently. I had worked hard at keeping appropriate boundaries to keep from falling in love with Becky. These boundaries hurt her deeply and didn't keep me from falling for her at all.

I looked around at all of my friends who were fighting against their same-gender orientation, and as I looked, I saw such misery! It wasn't working for anyone. Ten years earlier, Elaine was on a mission trip when a romantic relationship with a female peer was discovered by the program staff. The two were made to confess their "sin" publicly to the rest of the mission team. Within one year, Elaine was married. She spent over ten years in a marriage that was not satisfying. Now she seemed to be in a relationship that she couldn't even acknowledge. Becky had never lived more than two years in one state and claimed that every single one of her best friends had fallen in love with her, and suffered for it. Most of these friends came out as lesbian shortly after their friendship ended—for this Becky was both ashamed and perplexed. Jenny, the woman she loved most, was destroyed by depression and believed she would never recover from the loss of their relationship. And I was an emotional mess.

Meanwhile, my brother seemed to be enjoying a healthy, monogamous relationship with his partner. I'd become friends with a lesbian couple who seemed to have a healthy relationship and maintain a Christian identity. I could see that openly gay people were not at all like the miserable, broken people that ex-gay materials had portrayed. All that I had read about the misery of "the gay lifestyle" was not adding up with my own experience. Openly gay people seemed to be the happy ones, while I was suffering. As much as I tried to follow the *Pursuing Sexual Wholeness* path to spiritual healing, I could not balance both goals of making close friends and not letting them get too close. I began to wonder if it was possible that God would be okay with me being lesbian.

Six months before I shifted my views about homosexuality, I was at the lowest low of my life. Between the conflict with friends, the loss of my career, and the financial disaster, I sunk into my third bout with depression. I had become so anxious that I developed a large and visible nervous twitch. It was like I was being startled by my own thoughts; I'd jump out of my skin at the slightest provocation. I'd think of something mildly uncomfortable and my body would respond like it was just cattle-prodded.

This bizzare mental health symptom seemed to baffle my doctors, and it scared me to death. The embarrassment of this twitch made me want to hibernate at home alone. I had a growing interest in the mental health field, but I worried that twitching would keep me from being effective with my clients. Imagine seeing a therapist who jumped out of her skin every time you talked about your feelings! I feared that this twitch would take away another career and leave me with no hope at all.

Losing control of my body was deeply unsettling. I tried many different medications, took a battery of tests, and tried counseling, massage, acupunture, and exercise. Thankfully, it never did interfere with any work with clients or career aspirations. Over the next three years, as I was coming out, a mixture of medication, counseling, excercise, and general healthy living reduced the twitch to where it was almost gone. The twitch is still with me, but now it is so rare that most people don't know it's there. It is a battle scar from my year of losing everything and a small reminder of my previous unhappiness.

8

Impact: Conflict and Loss in Faith Communities

LEAVING A BELOVED CHURCH was a common and significant loss for many of my participants. Some left in protest over church teachings or because limitations were placed on their participation. Some were simply told they had to leave. Whatever the reason, they described the loss of their communities with terms like, "heartbroken," "devastated," and "crushed." The relationships they had formed at their churches were clearly important to them.

JACQUELINE: LOSS OF A BELOVED COMMUNITY

Jacqueline was referred to me by my mom, who knew her from Jacqueline's anti-bullying campaign work with PFLAG. Jacqueline and her partner lived in Minneapolis, and they adopted Amy (whose story appeared in the Violence chapter) through a program that sought to find families for LGBTQ homeless youth. I met Jacqueline for the interview in their Minneapolis home. Amy had asked in advance if she could stay and listen in on the interview. I agreed. Amy's "listening in" turned out to involve a fair amount of commentary, which led to a funny and touching interview with both of them.

Jacqueline and Amy seemed an unlikely match. Amy is conservative, Jacqueline is liberal; Amy is short, stocky, butch, and Latina, and Jacqueline is tall, lean, feminine, and blonde. Amy laughed throughout the interview, and Jacqueline was more likely to shed tears—usually when speaking of her love for Amy or her husband, Marcus. Jacqueline identifies as bisexual and has written a book about her experiences of loving her partner through his transition from female to male. After the transition, they were married.

Jacqueline grew up in a very liberal Catholic church in Milwaukee in the 1960s. Saint Boniface Church was active in the civil rights movement and organized community efforts to end racial segregation and poverty. Involvement in this church was a formative experience for Jacqueline. She seemed somewhat apologetic about her love of her early Catholic faith: "I always feel like I have to explain when I say that I was brought up Catholic. It's a really different version of Catholicism than what most people [know]. I did not go to Catholic school or any of that. It was very social justice [focused]. I've never been to confession."

Amy whispered, "That's the problem!"

Jacqueline was spared from most church-based condemnation of gay people. St. Boniface disbanded when she was about eight years old, so her family went to the home church of a Greek Orthodox minister who happened to be a gay man. It sounds like the family didn't know he was gay until later. Jacqueline recalled, "I have this vague memory of him being on TV and talking about gay stuff and saying that people think gay sex is something weird, and he was saying that we think straight sex is something weird." She remembers her father reacting with disgust and that they stopped attending the church after that. After leaving their Orthodox home church, Jacqueline's family stopped attending any religious services with any regularity.

As an adult, she attended seminary for a year, hoping to become a minister, but she became disillusioned with the ways the church discriminated against women. "That was one of my first experiences with discrimination. . . . This church that was championing equal rights when I was growing up is discriminating against me being a leader in the church. So I've experienced both the anti-gay and that anti-woman stuff from the church from two different places." Upon leaving seminary, she stayed away from organized religion for many years. "Later in my life, it was difficult to realize that the church wasn't standing up for all people, so [I] didn't go to church." Jacqueline returned to church when she was about thirty, after her grandmother's death. "I remember wandering in there in the middle of the snowstorm." She became a member of her neighborhood Catholic Church and stayed for twenty years.

Jacqueline came out as bisexual when she was about thirty-five. She started dating a woman that she'd met at church. "Part of what was complicated for me coming out, I am attracted to male energy in men and women. I like men, I'm very attracted to men, but then I'm attracted to this little subset of women."

Amy jumped in, "And Angelina Jolie."

Jacqueline laughed, "And Angelina Jolie; right, absolutely right. She's got a nice swagger to her."

Jacqueline's first same-gender relationship was celebrated in their community. Still, the church was under the authority of the greater Catholic Church, so the church celebrated certain things quietly and without allowing any printed material. "I remember I went to a lesbian commitment ceremony there. It was actually at [the church]. It was an underground thing, so that felt exciting. It's this weird mindset because you can get into this thing that were doing, this exciting, underground thing, which doesn't fully acknowledge that this underground thing shouldn't have to be underground. And what is the pain of that?"

After adopting Amy, the two attended mass together regularly. Eventually, Amy decided that she wanted to be confirmed. Jacqueline responded, "Oh, that's great honey." She added, "Then I realized I had never been confirmed! All of a sudden I was like, 'Whoops!'" So, they went through confirmation classes together.

The reality of the greater Catholic Church's views started to settle in for Jacqueline during the confirmation process.

> I was sitting in the class, and it hit me that my kid was gonna be—I can feel myself wanting to cry—confirmed in this church that was not gay affirming. And I knew it wasn't gay affirming. . . . That's the contradiction about being in a progressive Catholic Church: the congregation is very affirming, that wasn't a problem, but then you're connected to the larger church, which is not. So, it's easy to lull yourself into not thinking about it, but when you're sitting there in the class, you know. I had made my own peace with it. . . . I know what the church says about me and I don't care. So what? But it had a whole different resonance when it was Amy. And I want to cry, when it's about my kid. That's not okay.

Amy seemed touched and said, "You never talked to me about that."

Jacqueline disagreed, "I think we were driving. We always have good conversations when driving. I remember saying, 'Honey, you know what the Catholic Church says about gay people, right? I don't know if I can join.'"

She turned to Amy to remind her, "I quote this in the book honey! You said, 'Don't think about it as joining the church; think about it as standing up for the Lord.' Words of wisdom."

Amy agreed, "Sounds pretty great."

They decided to get confirmed together. Shortly thereafter a new conflict with the church developed. Jacqueline's partner, Marcus, had made the decision to transition from female to male, and they were planning to get married. Jacqueline wanted to celebrate these events with some form of religious ceremony. She explained, "As a Catholic, that whole ritual thing is really important. . . . I felt strongly that these events that were happening were events in which I needed my faith. I was going to be married. I wasn't *not* gonna be married in church. That felt important to me, to have a God presence there in my marriage, for my marriage. For the transition too, I wasn't gonna do that without having some sort of blessing. Obviously I wasn't doing the transition, but I needed that around the transition."

Jacqueline got the idea for a blessing while sitting in church, listening to the blessings said over other people. "They do blessings for the snowbirds going down to Florida. I thought, 'Well heck, this transition is a lot bigger deal than spending the winter in Florida; we ought to be able to do some sort of blessing for that, don't you think?'"

Marcus attended a congregational church that was active in LGBTQ advocacy work and was vocal about inclusion. Jacqueline was struck by the differences between how the two churches responded to Jacqueline and Marcus's request for a blessing.

> I talked to the priest first. . . . It really highlighted the difference in attitude between the underground mentality: we should be just grateful for whatever versus being open. At [the Catholic Church] the priest was like, "We can do the blessing, but we're gonna do it off to the side. It won't be part of anything; don't tell anybody." Marcus did not respond well to that. And I was like, "That's so cool that he's gonna find a way to do it at all!" That's where I was; sure, we'll go hide in the little corner here, as long as we can do it. Marcus could not relate to that, so we did it at [the congregational church].

Comparing the two churches, Jacqueline began to wonder, "What would it be like to be in an open situation?" One moment stood out to her at the congregational church. She said, "I could cry right now just think-ing about it; seeing in the bulletin where it says births and deaths. [The church] printed, 'Transition: Margery becomes Marcus.'" She paused as she got choked up and added, "It was like, Whoa! We're not hiding anything here. You know what I mean? What is there to hide? Here it is: Margery is Marcus; we want everybody to know! It's a good thing!"

As they were planning their wedding, Jacqueline tried to find out what the Catholic Church had to say about transgender people:

> My initial thought was they probably haven't gotten around to condemning transgender people yet, so we could probably get married. It took a lot of work to find out what the church said. . . . There's something that you call a "*sub secretum* document," which means in Latin "under secrecy." There's a Catholic news service article you can find on the Internet about this *sub secretum* docu-ment that was distributed to all the bishops, which basically says that you are the gender you are when you were born and baptized because you can't be baptized in the wrong gender. So if you have a transgender transition, that is evidence of mental instability be-cause you really can only be the body you appear to be when you were born, and if you're mentally unstable then of course you're not fit to be married, among other things.

Jacqueline described how this information affected her: "When I found that out, it was devastating. I cannot tell you how painful it was. I could not set my foot back at [my church]. Even though they would've been [accepting], it wasn't about them; it was about the fact that this church community that I've been a part of for twenty years—I would not be able to be married there. This was my community, this was my faith community, and I was a regular churchgoer for twenty years there. It was devastating."

Amy and Jacqueline discussed one challenge in being a part of this church, which was being careful not to expose the affirming leaders to negative repercussions; this showed their respect and love for these leaders. Amy said, "I think Father ___ did the best he could do, I think he was pretty phenomenal for being supportive."

Jacqueline agreed, "He absolutely was, and he could only go so far." She added, "That's part of what happens: you're put in this position, are you gonna put the priest in danger of losing his job? Or being excommuni-cated? Or losing his pension? How far are you gonna push it? You like him, he's a good man; are you gonna do that to him?"

Amy added, "Well, then the other douche bag became priest."

Jacqueline yelled, "This is being taped, Amy!" She explained, "Things kind of went downhill."

Jacqueline has been attending the Baptist church with Amy and enjoys it but doesn't feel like it is her church—one that reflects her Catholic heritage. In describing her current faith she said, "I do feel wounded. It's been difficult. . . . I haven't had a church home, and it's been painful for me. It's been really painful." Despite all this, Jacqueline still believes in the loving God she learned about in her early days at St. Boniface. I asked each of my participants if their view of God has changed since their early years. Jacqueline responded, "Has my view of God changed? Probably not. I believe in a benevolent, loving God. It seems like I should say I've had some profound thing, but when it comes down to it, the God of my childhood is the God I still believe in. In some ways I feel like I'm cursed by that because I am, at my core, this activist person who believes that we are called to engage in the world and do what we can to make the world a better place. So I'm always tilting at windmills and continuing to believe."

AMY: "I FEEL HEARTBROKEN THAT I AM NOT WELCOME HERE"

Amy also had the painful experience of losing a beloved church. She had felt such a strong connection to the Lutheran church of her early teenage years, and she had experienced such grief over losing it, that she went back with Jacqueline years later, "just to see what it was like." She found no encouragement there. "The pastor was different, the message was the same. I went with my mom, Jacqueline, and she was all emotional about it. I'm like, 'Calm down!' (Laughs.) She was mad at the church because of their message, and it was the church that I loved. But I'm like, 'We don't want to start anything! I just want to see what it's like now.' I do miss it. Still, I do feel a lot of hurt about it." The pastor never said anything about homosexuality during the sermon on that visit, but it was still clear to her that "the message was the same" because of how they were treated as visitors:

> People were curious about us. . . . I was in a shirt and a tie—that's probably what it was to be honest (laughing). They were like, "Who are these people?" We ended up getting into a conversation, and I could tell my mom was getting a little worked up. They were just asking questions. . . . "How did you hear about us?" "Why are you here?" I'm like, "I used to come here as a kid." And they were

like, "So why did you leave?" And, I really couldn't say. It just felt
too vulnerable for me. Then my mom didn't really know how to
answer, so it just seemed like we were spies (laughing). After that,
people locked up. They weren't very welcoming. And they were
like, "We're very Bible-based, and we believe certain passages that
a lot of other Lutheran churches don't believe." What was interesting is that they were coming up again for a vote to break off from
the ELCA [Evangelical Lutheran Church in America] that Sunday.
They didn't really say it's because of the gay issue. It was just really
weird on both of our parts not knowing how to communicate. I
wish I could've talked to them and said, "This is a church that I
loved, and I feel heartbroken that I am not welcome here." Not that
they would've cared necessarily because I'm Satan's daughter to
them (laughing), like I'm there to convert their children. (Laughs.)

I can relate to the heartbreak that both Amy and Jacqueline experienced as they left their churches. When it came time to leave my church, I
was certain that it was the right time and the right thing to do. I left feeling
righteous anger, but I was unprepared for the grief that came with leaving.
Losing my church was a huge loss. I still feel left out of something special
and irreplaceable. (More of my story with my church is still to come.) Hannah gives another perspective on being queer within the same community.

HANNAH: IT'S EASY TO PRETEND

I would have never thought to talk to Hannah about my project. She and
her husband attended my (previous) church with their young child. I didn't
know them well, but they seemed like one of many young couples at our
church; I made assumptions that she was more conservative and more
straight than what was actually true. She told me about her college days
and her involvement in LGBTQ advocacy groups and that she identifies as
bisexual. Hannah feels a strong pull to be silent about her sexual orientation at church and "pretend" to be straight, which she describes as "not
very fulfilling." Her perspective opened my eyes to some of the complexity
involved in being bisexual in a faith community and elsewhere. Hannah
is quiet, kind, unassuming, and thoughtful. She is devoted to her family
and continues to struggle with how to be herself among her conservative
friends.

Hannah grew up in a Catholic church where her dad was a deacon. She
described what this means, saying, "You know how Catholics believe that

you actually change the bread and the wine into the body and the blood—
he can't do that, but he can lead an entire service minus communion." Her
father would often give the homily at their church, and he presided over her
wedding and baptized her daughter.

> When I was young, I had this unwavering faith. It was like: God is
> what he is, and I'm fine with it. I felt like I had a good relationship
> with God. And then I was fourteen, and I was going through con-
> firmation and everyone around me was just going through it like
> sheep. Nobody [was being] confirmed because they really wanted
> to affirm that they were making a commitment to life with God;
> they just did it because that's what your parents make you do, and
> that's what you do when you're fourteen and Catholic—you get
> confirmed.

Hannah's first conflict with the church was not about sexual orientation but about church leaders' dismissal of sexual violence. Even with her
father's position as one in authority at the church, Hannah was not supported by other church leaders when another member sexually assaulted
her.

> I was dating a boy who turned out to be really abusive, and I lost
> my virginity nonconsensually. He was in my confirmation class. It
> was this big, messy ordeal. I had to tell my parents what happened;
> I had to get a restraining order—crazy nuts-ness for a fourteen-
> year-old. I went to my confirmation leader, and I was like, "This
> boy is abusing me; I don't feel safe being in this room with him. I
> really want to be confirmed, but I can't do it with him here." She
> basically told me that if I can't handle being in the same room with
> him that I don't need to be confirmed. So I quit, and it started a
> several year–long crisis of faith for me. Understandably so, if one
> of your spiritual leaders is like, "It's okay that your boyfriend raped
> you; buck up."

The rape, as well as its aftermath, profoundly impacted her spiritual
and emotional well-being. "I became very staunchly anti-church, very angry at God. And it was that way for a long time. I think I got to the point
where I went from angry to slightly agnostic. I don't think I ever would've
considered myself an atheist, but I went through a long period of time
where I questioned if God existed, and if God existed why he was such a
prick."

During her college years, she came out as bisexual and got involved
in LGBTQ advocacy groups on campus. It wasn't until several years after

college when she was married and planning a family that she renewed her interest in finding a faith community. "I felt something was missing. The common thread among all of my atheist, weird, pot-smoking friends—they were all really angry. There was a lot of bitterness and 'proud otherness,' and a lot of my faith-based friends seemed to be happier. A lot of that is perception; it's what people choose to project, but my friends who had a strong belief in God were never vocally angry about the world. And my friends who didn't, generally were. So that made me think that this is a piece I need to explore."

Hannah and her husband went in search of a church. "We went to Vineyard, which I thought was a cult because I knew [a friend there], and whenever something was wrong in someone's life she would be like, 'Just pray about it;' and everything would be okay. I hated that. My friend's ex-something-or-other wasn't paying child support, and she said, 'Just pray about it.' And I was like, 'No! Go to the county!' I was mad. So I [thought], 'I don't want to be around those God people because they are crazy.'"

Something changed Hannah's mind. "We went and it was a really good sermon, and I felt super moved." They ended up staying for more than three years. As Hannah began to connect with others at her new church, she didn't feel comfortable bringing her whole self to the community. Since she is in a heterosexual marriage, she found it easy to hide or pretend at church that she is not bisexual—though she wishes she didn't have to hide. She doesn't tell her church friends about a past relationship with a woman or about her involvement in a gay rights group on campus, nor does she tell others that she identifies as bisexual. She fears what it would mean for her and her family if the church really knew these things. "It's really easy for me to 'not' be bisexual—I'm making quote signs right now. It's easy to 'not' be bisexual at church because I'm not visibly queer—I have a husband. You look at me, [and assume] I'm straight, so it's easy for me to pretend. But it's not very fulfilling to pretend."

It is not fulfilling to hide major pieces of you, not fulfilling to put up a fake front, and not fulfilling to hide your past. Hannah was making strong connections at the church but still felt the need to hide because of church politics and culture.

> I found out that in being queer you can't teach or preach. That was something I was considering. It made me mad that as of right now I could because they would just assume. But I would be lying. If I was like, "Guess what? I'm bisexual." Would they be like,

"You can't do this anymore"? It's frustrating . . . I love that the sign says "Everybody is welcome." You're welcome to come, but you're not welcome to actually have a hand in anyone's faith formation. [It] bothers me that because of your sexuality somehow you don't know God as well or you can't teach about God. What do [they] think, that you're going to be handing out the gay agenda? That makes me mad to know that I could do anything I wanted to do right now as far as participation, but if I was open about who I was, I wouldn't be able to.

Hannah reflected back on times when she was able to be more open, saying, "I was very out in college and it made me happy. I led Alliance, I was active in the community, but then I left my liberal bubble where it was okay." One other difference is that now she considers how her decisions affect her whole family. "Even in St. Cloud it wasn't fully okay to be out. It was okay to be out in certain circles. But I didn't give a shit. I'm like, 'Whatever, I don't care what you think.' Now I've got more at stake because [of] my kid. She's little enough that she won't remember. But my kid is friends with other people's kids, so their negative attitudes towards me have an effect on my daughter."

At the time of the interview, Hannah was getting tired of hiding and was starting to be more open about herself and her beliefs with those who disagree. She talked a bit about her current faith, saying, "I believe that God is always present in our lives and that God will try to help us find the right path, that God has made us all unique and given us free will to screw up, and to try different things, and ask questions."

She elaborated on the importance of asking questions in order to grow spiritually instead of blindly accepting what other Christians say is true. "My central theme around faith is that God just loves; God wants us to love each other, so we shouldn't be squabbling over theoretical differences and whose ideology is correct. We should just love each other and leave the details to God. And I do think that God is speaking to us if we are willing to listen."

This belief that God would speak to her was a new and important development in her faith. "In the beginning, [I thought], 'You're supposed to do what God wants.' Now I am, like, 'Are you sure this is what you want me to do?' Having a dialogue with God—that's something I've never had in my past; I feel like the relationship is reciprocal. . . . If you're listening, God will offer advice or support."

Hannah's experience in our church involved both connection to other believers and connection at a distance. She hears God speak to her when she is at church, *and* she feels unfulfilled in hiding from others. Because I know her church well, part of me thinks that if she were to come out as bisexual, she would find much more support there than she imagines, especially because she is in a monogamous heterosexual marriage. I also think that pushing too hard for inclusion of LGBTQ people may not go well for her.

The women I interview were all impacted by messages about homosexuality in so many different ways. From violence, to homelessness, to depression, to significant losses of relationships and communities, they were all harmed by oppressive and pervasive cultural dynamics. Each woman embarked on a process of tearing apart and rebuilding the faith she'd been handed and developing spiritual beliefs and practices that allow her to bring her whole self to God and to others. This process of reclaiming faith should already be apparent in the stories told so far. The following chapters highlight more of the process and the results of the fight to hold onto faith.

9

Reclamation: Integration and Wholeness

UNTIL THIS POINT, THE focus of this book has been on the harm done by Christian groups who have promoted inaccurate and inflammatory messages about lesbian and bisexual women. While each individual story has a relatively happy ending, the focus of each chapter has been on the ways Christian churches have caused harm to queer people. When I started this research, it was important to me to find people who had held onto faith. I needed to know that there were others who'd figured out a way to be both gay and Christian, and I wanted to know how they did it. I wondered if staying in the church was hurting me more than it was helping me, so I went in search of those who have gone before me (or at least alongside me). I needed to know that I wasn't crazy for wanting to remain a Christian. From this point forward in the book, the focus shifts away from the harm done and towards the ways in which these women have integrated their spiritual beliefs and sexual orientation, and the ways they've benefitted from finding an integrated and authentic life.

There is no formula for people who wish to make peace with their sexual orientation and a belief system that condemns same-gender relationships. Formulas are of little use in spiritual matters. Each person I interviewed took a different winding road in their process of integrating their faith and sexuality. One major theme was that each woman needed to find a way to make her faith her own. This involved rejecting some of what she had been taught and seeking out truth for herself. This is the essence of James Fowler's description of adult faith (Stage 4), moving away from complete trust in spiritual authorities and going through the "angst and struggle" of asking big questions and forming one's own belief system. Some never make it to Stage 4 faith and remain dependent on the authorities of their own spiritual culture.[1] Those who have been rejected by the church are thrown into a spiritual crisis that can either lead to self-condemnation or substantial spiritual growth.

This growth stems from conflict. For some of my participants, the conflict was purely external; they never believed that it was wrong to be lesbian or bisexual. For them, seeking integration involved deciphering how they wanted to respond to spiritual authorities and institutions that rejected or condemned them. Others struggled internally with teachings and Bible verses that seemed to oppose same-gender relationships as they sought to do what was right in the eyes of God. Everyone had to resolve conflict about their association with the Christian church and all of its baggage.

NEVER AN ISSUE

My church experiences led me to believe that pursuing a relationship with a woman would be outside of God's plan. Most people in my Christian circles felt the same way. As I started my research, I imagined that most women from nonaffirming environments would have struggled with this internal conflict like I did. Among my participants, only half internalized the belief that same-gender relationships were against God's will. Four women (Jacqueline, Maureen, Gretchen, and Hannah) reported that they never believed that it was wrong to be gay. Some said they knew that their church believed homosexual relationships were wrong, but they dismissed this idea because of a deeper internal sense of morality. Maureen, while in an argument with her in-laws, said "I've never felt like I was doing something wrong." She showed trust in an internal compass that could help her know right from wrong. When asked about internal conflict regarding being bisexual and Catholic, Jacqueline seemed almost confused and said, "It was never an issue."

Hearing my participants' stories made it clear to me how much the church is responsible for instilling shame and guilt in LGBTQ people. The women who did not hear overt negative messages in their churches were able to dismiss the idea that their religious authorities claim it's wrong to be gay. For those who were exposed to consistent condemning messages

1. Fowler, *Stages of Faith*, 182.

at their churches, they were more likely to take on beliefs that they were damaged or flawed. Both Laurie and I recall a time, before our exposure to evangelical Christianity, when we never believed it was wrong to be gay. After "finding God" in these environments and getting involved with near manic intensity, we both ended up in reparative therapy of one form or another. It speaks to me of God's laws being "written on our hearts," as it says in Romans, that our consciences can testify to God and truth. Culturally bound church teachings can get in the way of what we know to be true.

RETURN TO THE BIBLE

Protestantism has often relied on the principle of *sola Scriptura* ("by Scripture alone")—that the Bible holds all the knowledge we need for finding truth and living rightly. While this principle has some problems (for example, it is impossible to interpret Scripture outside of the lens of our own culture; Scripture has been used for all sorts of evil; and the Holy Spirit ought to have a role in discernment of truth), the importance of the Bible to the Christian faith is immeasurable. For all Christians, it is our sacred text, full of rich imagery, powerful stories, and challenging directives, as well as history, mystery, and poetry. In short, it is of vital importance to our faith. It is not surprising that the first thing many women did in the process of integrating their spiritual and sexual identities was to "go back to the Bible." Before they could do anything else, they needed to read again what the Bible really said about homosexuality and other issues. They needed to see the context behind the words, understand the language of the original text, or see for themselves the passages others had quoted at them. Ericka, Amy, Laurie, Gretchen, and Kimberly all talked about deeper study of the Bible to "see what it really said."

My Story: The Truth of the Bible

I, too, needed to reconcile with the Bible before I could believe that God was okay with me dating women. After facing the truth that my try-not-to-be-gay life was unhealthy, I started to rethink my beliefs. At first, I thought along the lines of culture; Abraham had many wives, as did David, Solomon, and other forefathers of the faith. All the Christians I knew would say that polygamy is wrong, yet God worked within the culture of these men and used them to do great and amazing things as they led the people of God. Maybe God could still use me, love me, and work through me if my culture said that it was acceptable to be with a woman. I was still buying into the idea of my wrong-ness but wondered if it was something God could work with. As I began to pursue this idea, I was in awe at the ways I experienced God telling me that not only could he work with me but that he created me just as I am. God spoke through Scripture, friends, strangers, and even a very timely fortune cookie that read, "Who can give a law to lovers? Love is a greater gift unto itself."

On one occasion, I was approached by a woman from my church who had recently moved here from Brazil. She was known to have a prophetic gift in her ability to pray for others. At the Vineyard, we sometimes joked that people with this mysterious gift can "read your mail" because, like it or not, they seem to know all about your current personal struggles. It seems there are certain people who can be supernaturally insightful in their prayers for others. I've encountered a few people who have this gift; when they've prayed for me, I've been dumbfounded and moved to tears. This particular woman told me in broken English that she thought God wanted her to share a Bible passage with me. She told me that she sensed my loneliness and had been praying for me to find a marriage partner. She said that my partnership would not look like other people's because I was not like other people. . . . I was different. She had me read a passage from the book of Revelation; it is a message to the church in the ancient city of Philadelphia. It reads:

> This is the message from the one who is holy and true, the one who has the key of David. What he opens, no one can close; and what he closes, no one can open: I know all the things you do, and I have opened a door for you that no one can close. You have little strength, yet you obeyed my word and did not deny me. Look, I will force those who belong to Satan's synagogue—those liars who say they are Jews but are not—to come and bow down at your feet. They will acknowledge that you are the ones I love. (Rev. 3:7–9 NLT)

As I read the words aloud, I could barely choke them out over my tears. A new door was being opened for me. It seemed as if God was saying that a life of possibilities was before me—not a life of impossible rules. I knew that the door opened before me was a door to a new life and new relationships. I felt that God was acknowledging that other people wanted to shut doors but that God was and is the only one who could open them for me. The last lines gripped me as well. To me, it meant that all people who claim to be children of God while they promote religious bigotry will fall at our feet with apology and acknowledge that we are loved by God. What a beautiful idea.

This passage was the prophetic message to the church in a city called "Brotherly Love." Apparently they were loved by God while others used religion to claim otherwise. (Some things haven't changed in two thousand years.) One thing I've seen through this research project is that God still steps in and speaks hope, life, and love to the people whom the church has rejected. Getting kicked out of church is damaging and painful, but it can't keep God from revealing love to the outcasts. This passage says to me that there will come a day when everyone will see how much we are all loved by God.

Despite many signs that pointed me toward the possibility of a relationship with a woman, I had a hard time figuring out what to do about biblical passages that seemed to condemn homosexuality. In my searching for direction, I went on a three-day silent retreat to a hermitage called Pacem in Terris. Translated "Peace on Earth," Pacem is a place designed for people to get away from their busy lives and responsibilities in order to spend time alone with God. As I drove into the woods of their site, I was moved to tears by the sense of peace that came over me. I felt as if this was truly a holy place that lived up to its name.

At the hermitage, I spent forty-eight hours in silence equipped with my Bible, a journal, and some walking shoes. I read over all of the passages that address homosexuality, finding many of them irrelevant. Still, there were a couple New Testament passages that I found difficult to dismiss. As I read through Romans 1, I continued past the passages addressing homosexuality and found a passage that forever changed my view of Scripture. Paul was addressing the first Christians, who were Jewish, and was calling for the inclusion of gentile believers into fellowship. After spending a paragraph pointing out the sins of the gentiles, Paul turns the tables and says, "You are the same." He goes on:

> You who call yourselves Jews are relying on God's law, and you boast about your special relationship with him. You know what he wants; you know what is right because you have been taught his law. You are convinced that you are a guide for the blind and a light for people who are lost in darkness. You think you can instruct the ignorant and teach children the ways of God. *For you are certain that God's law gives you complete knowledge and truth.* Well, then,

if you teach others, why don't you teach yourself? (Rom. 2:17–21
NLT, emphasis added)

I thought to myself how Christians (myself included) have relied on
God's law and assumed that having the law gave "complete knowledge and
truth." I began to wonder if maybe the Bible could be truth, but not the
whole truth . . . that the Spirit is the one who guides us into all truth. The
Spirit certainly seemed to be talking to me. I walked away from my silent
retreat with a new sense of God's blessing in my decision to come out.

Still another experience impacted me during this time. Shortly after
my silent retreat, a woman from church offered to pray for me. She thought
she was praying about how I'd found it hard to hear from God, but her
words had a very different meaning to me. She said, "I feel like God is saying that you think that there is something wrong with you, and you think
that is why you are this way. He wants you to know that there is nothing
wrong with you. He says 'This is how I made you and it's beautiful!'" These
words have stuck with me, telling me that I'm not broken, damaged, or anything less than what I should be. I remember these words whenever people
talk about the claims of ex-gay ministries or the "sin" of homosexuality.

I was amazed by all the ways God seemed to be speaking to me, saying, "This is how I made you," "I've opened a new door for you," "No law
can hold the whole truth," and "My spirit will guide you." The idea that God
speaks to us was commonly taught in my Christian communities. I had
heard from God in this way many times before, but I'd never experienced
God saying that being gay was "beautiful." I was undone.

It was surprising to me how reading or rereading the Bible led many of
the women in my study to move towards a more affirming faith. Studying
the Bible freed them from a sense of condemnation and gave them deeper
understanding of the context of passages that get used against them. They
derived meaning from what they read and found it applicable to their lives.
The Bible ceased to be a barrier to an affirming faith.

OTHER SPIRITUAL PRACTICES

In addition to studying the Bible, developing personal spiritual practices
was a part of each person's faith journey. For Ericka it was a twelve-step
group and time alone in the wilderness; Laurie went to seminary and spent
her mornings with God; Renae sought mentors; and Maureen surrounded
herself with quotes and Bible verses—daily reminders of Scripture and

God's love. These practices provided comfort, guidance, and reassurance in the midst of challenging times and helped them feel connected to a loving God.

GRETCHEN: "YOU GO INSIDE TO COME OUT"

Gretchen's story illustrates how spirituality can be a source of guidance, support, and resilience even in the coming-out process. Gretchen and I were introduced at a PFLAG meeting. After I had completed my research for my MSW project, I was given the opportunity to speak on a faith panel during one of PFLAG's weekly meetings. I had low expectations because PFLAG is my mom's thing, and I thought it would be . . . well . . . lame. Instead, the stories of the other panel speakers were inspiring, and I met wonderful people with whom I still keep in contact. Gretchen serves on the PFLAG board of directors because of her desire to give back by helping parents support their LGBTQ kids. We met for the interview at a St. Paul café after work. Her story was a little different than the others in that she did not have a strong religious upbringing. Gretchen said,

> My father was in the military during the Vietnam War. My mom took us to church in the chapel on the base. My brother and I were baptized, but I can't honestly say I remember spending any time in church as a young person at all, except during the times when I'd go visit my grandparents. . . . My southern grandmother went to the Southern Methodist Church, and my grandmother in Minnesota was a First Congregationalist. . . . I had an unconventional upbringing. When my parents got divorced, I was four, my brother was six; instead of one parent raising us, they split us apart; so my mom raised me and my dad raised my brother. We lived fairly close together for the first ten years or so. We did the every other weekend thing. Neither one of my parents were involved in communities of faith. Being with our extended families was the only time that my brother and I had any exposure to church. We would go to Sunday school when we were either in Minnesota or Oklahoma, so we learned all the songs that kids learn, like "Jesus Loves Me." But we didn't really have much of what I would call a really strong faith upbringing. My real connection was when I got a little bit older.

Gretchen explained how exposure to the faith of her extended family provided her with positive examples of authentic faith:

> I would usually spend my summers with my mom's family in Oklahoma. My mom's sisters were deeply devout women, and I always went to church with them. They lived who they were—they were amazing, loving, caring women. . . . During the week we would make deliveries to food banks or we'd go to the big farmers' markets near the end of the summer and buy huge amounts of corn and staples, and we would deliver them to churches. . . . . That was really a meaningful thing to me.

Gretchen was moved by the faith of her aunts, who lived out a generosity and care for the poor and hungry. Having these examples painted a very positive picture of what faith and spirituality could be.

This faith turned out to be a much-needed source of strength for Gretchen to get through her teenage years. She and her brother grew up in Washington State, and then she and her mom moved to Florida when she was twelve. "I was raised on an island in the Puget Sound. . . . It was an amazing, beautiful place, and I was surrounded by this incredible beauty my entire life. Then we moved to Florida, and I was now away from my dad and my brother; and it was just my mom and I. Everything was foreign to me; I felt like people were really judgmental."

Gretchen described herself as a tomboy, and she didn't feel like she fit in at the school in Florida. When she was in high school, her mom traveled a lot, leaving her home alone. She was isolated and struggling and knew she needed to move back to Washington to be with her dad.

> I was at this crossroads in my life. As an adult I look back and I say, "You know, it could've gone either way." I could've been one of those kids that could've fallen into depression that could've taken my life. But, because I took the time to call my dad and say, "Dad, I don't want to be here anymore." My dad [said], "I've got a ticket in the mail for you." It was that very act by my dad [that] gave me enough faith—I call it faith now, but at the time I didn't—gave me hope that maybe. . . . That side that I felt was so dark and so heavy. . . . I felt like I was standing right on the edge of the cliff, and I just [had to] take a step back. . . . Those are the moments that I look back on. That was when God was saying, "Hang on. You may have something to learn from this."

Gretchen returned to Washington and felt a new freedom to be herself. She took up spiritual practices that facilitated her coming out, and her depression lifted. Strangely enough, she took an interest in theology at the height of the AIDS crisis when certain Christians were claiming that AIDS was God's judgment on gay people.

> I had pretty strong political feelings about what I call "the church." I knew enough about what I was seeing on TV that I absolutely abhorred the institution. I was seeing all of these televangelists. You had Jimmy Swaggart and Tammy Faye and [Jim] Bakker on TV . . . saying horrible things about our community. [It] was the culture wars and, "the gays are trying to destroy our community." So, here I was developing this sense of spirituality; I had this deep sense of spirituality, [and] I had the sense that the Christian church (to me there was no difference between Baptists and Catholics; they're all saying the same thing) hated me. They were saying that God was killing my brothers and sisters, and to me that was unconscionable. It was terrible. There's no way I was gonna engage in a community of faith because to me there wasn't such a thing. It didn't exist.

The behavior of these Christians nearly turned her off from spiritual interests, but she continued to study theology out of her own curiosity. Gretchen started practicing meditation at the age of sixteen, just after moving back to Washington, as she was emerging from depression and coming out to herself. "That's what my journey was about; you go inside to come out. That's what I learned from Thich Nhat Hanh." She started a regular practice of walking and meditating along the shores of Puget Sound.

> I would go to the beach, park my car in the parking lot, and I would walk for two miles down the beach and two miles back. It was all about breathing and clearing your mind. Whatever comes in comes in, and you let it go out, being completely at peace with where you are and focusing on your breathing. I would come back from those walks, and I would feel such a sense of peace, and a sense of solace, and a sense of safety that I had never felt in my entire life. Growing up in a split family and not feeling a lot of security, that was a really big deal. Coming out was easy because, in those moments, you have these thoughts that come into your head and you accept them and you let them go. Like, "That girl—I really like her. Okay Gretchen, feel that and let it go." [Or], "I'm pretty sure that I'm gay. Okay, that's okay, now let that go." So there wasn't any real battle that I had with it because I went through this spiritual journey at the same time. I was practicing to accept the spiritual side of me while I was coming to accept what my identity was as a person.

The depth of spirituality Gretchen spoke about was impressive. She had a profound spiritual life as a teenage girl. Her meditation practices were integral to her process of self-acceptance and to coming out at a young age.

In addition to walking meditations on the beach, Gretchen also searched out books on religion and theology. She was curious about the origins of Christianity and drawn to some of the early Christian teachings.

> I had started reading the Bible because I wanted to actually know what it said. They were saying it said all these things, but it did not actually say that. I went to the bookstore and there's all these books about Hebrew interpretations, Greek interpretations, and all these great theological studies that were being done on the true language of Scripture and what was really going on there and then. You had these books about gnosticism and the origins of Christianity, and how are these things connected—that was all fascinating. To me, that's what Christianity became; all these other people were just a bunch of politicians that were trying to grab power. They were trying to influence the community by demonizing [us] and saying horrible things that were leading to the death of innocent people. I had a really hard time reconciling that, but those things were separate. Delving into theological ideas and concepts—which is what all the great theologians have always done—I loved that!

Reading theology and practicing meditation allowed Gretchen to develop a spiritual life in the early '80s, despite the prevalence of Christian-inspired hateful messages about LGBTQ people and despite her own disgust at their claims.

Still, she felt lonely in her spiritual life and wanted to find others who shared these interests with her. "I really struggled to find gays and lesbians who were willing to talk about the things that I was reading." Her friends did not share these interests and didn't care to talk with her about them. "All my gay friends thought that I was the biggest nerd on the planet because I like to read this stuff."

It wasn't until she joined the military that she found others who shared her spiritual interests.

> I was in college for about a year and a half and I was struggling. I couldn't figure out what I wanted to be in life, so I left and worked for a year. [I] knew that I wanted to engage in service, so I joined the military. I spent four years in the Army, most of that time in Germany. I was fortunate to have that group of friends that come from all walks of life, from all over the country, and have really

diverse experiences. One of my good friends was raised a staunch Catholic from Southern California. She was an amazing person and was one of my dearest friends while I was in the Army. She was one of these people that love to talk about theology and religion and had taken her own journey.

They spent their breakfasts together every morning and often talked about matters of faith. Together, they began to draw connections between serving in the church and serving in the military.

> She would talk about what it was like growing up Catholic. [Our dialogue] wasn't so much about faith as it was really about being two lesbians, both engaging in institutions that we weren't technically allowed to be a part of, but we believed in. Sitting there in our camouflage uniforms, getting ready to go do our job—we did this for a number of years. It occurred to me that I couldn't allow this outside institution [the church], which didn't technically exist as an institution, dictate my relationship. That's what I took out of those discussions, being able to juxtapose the idea that I was involved in an institution that I believed in and served what I saw as a higher good.

After serving in Germany, Gretchen moved to Fort Bliss in El Paso because the woman she was dating was transferred there. Gretchen got involved in a predominantly gay church in El Paso known as the MCC (Metropolitan Community Church).

> It was a wonderful, wonderful place. It was a largely Hispanic and very Catholic community, but there was a ton of gays and lesbians. . . . We only lived there for two years but we got involved in this MCC church and there was about 150 to 200 regular members. [They] did Bible study and all sorts of fun things together, and they were people that came from every sort of religious institution that you could imagine; it was crazy. All these people were sitting together and we were able to worship together. I had finally come to this place, but it was like, "This is it! This is what I need!" I was almost instantly comfortable there. . . . They let me sing in the chorus even though I cannot carry a tune in a bucket. It was such a joyous experience for me. It was so amazing to hear other people who had not given up. They knew that they had been called, no matter how horrible their stories were. And mine wasn't a horrible story by any stretch of the imagination, but no matter how horrible their stories were, they always felt like God had said, "Just hang on."

Taking part in this church led Gretchen to a lifelong commitment to engage in faith communities. Despite many moves across the country, she always looked for a church home. She said, "No matter where I've lived, . . . I've always found communities of faith that were open and affirming. I was not willing to settle for anything else."

When she first moved to Minnesota, it took Gretchen nearly two years to find a church that felt right to her. She said, "Minnesotans are just a little different," referring to Minnesota's culture of polite and guarded distance, compared to the openness of the South and the West Coast. Eventually she found a church she liked:

> I was there for fifteen minutes, and I knew I was home. It's kind of like looking for a house to buy: you look at a bazillion houses and you walk into this house and it's like this house was built for you. Your heart falls on the floor the moment you're there. That's the way I felt. It's a musical liturgy and it's high church, you know, it's really formal, but it's so amazing! It's in a fairly poor neighborhood on Chicago. Walking in there and finding that place, I knew that the journey that I had taken up to that point had taken me to a truly amazing place. I knew that I had just found a church; that I had found a home. Really, it is my home. All of the people there, they are my brothers and sisters. They're my family.

At that point in her life Gretchen had never found a partner who shared her spiritual interests. She didn't really believe it was possible.

> I've chronically dated people for years; dated someone for a year and a half [to] two years, and these topics of spirituality come up, and it's like [they say], "No, that's just not for me." My cousin said to me one day—it was probably one of the most difficult things she ever said—she said, "Gretchen, let me give you a piece of advice. Never consider a long-term relationship with someone who doesn't share your relationship with God." Now that's a pretty funny thing for your lesbian cousin to say to you. That's just not something you hear. And, I was like, "Well, fat chance. That's not gonna happen."

Then Gretchen met Kat. Actually, she'd known Kat for over a year through work, but one day they saw each other differently:

> She and I work for the same company. . . . One day, I don't know what it was, something in the air, and we saw each other. We started dating, and I took her to a women's hockey game—not terribly

romantic. After we'd gone out a couple of times, I said, "I was wondering if you'd be interested in going to church with me?," because I thought she was amazing. I'd known her for a year and a half. I knew who she was, and I knew that was gonna be the deal breaker. There was something about what my cousin said to me that stuck in my head. [Kat] said, "I would love to go to church with you." . . . So I took her; and we sat there and she had tears in her eyes, and she said, "It has been so many years since I have been in a place that I felt safe." She certainly has her own story, but she fell in love with it and we fell in love. The church has been absolutely central to our relationship and our faith in God. And what Jesus calls us to do is central to our marriage. She is now the treasurer on our church vestry, which actually takes up a lot more of her time than I thought it would.

Gretchen laughed at this and joked that she didn't need Kat to like the church quite *that* much.

Kat and Gretchen traveled to Iowa and got legally married before it was legal in Minnesota. Still, their church was involved and did a blessing. Gretchen recalled, "Our pastor said, 'If you're gonna get married, then you need to do marriage counseling.'" Her pastor expected them to do the same marriage counseling the church required of any straight couple. Gretchen said:

> It was really intense, and it was super interesting, and we learned a ton. We truly do have a community of faith around us, and it's amazing. I feel so incredibly blessed; every day I'm reminded that God brings so many other people into my life. Like your folks! They're so full of love and energy but people of deep faith. Those are the things that drive me. I find that the older I get the less anger I feel about things. I feel impassioned by them, but I feel a lot less anger because I realize that anger is really destructive for me.

I find Gretchen and Kat's story incredibly touching (not just because they love my parents). The church became central to their relationship, and they have stayed connected to it. Gretchen spoke passionately about her belief in the beautiful potential of faith communities. She described her own investment, saying, "I've realized that the more engaged I become with a community of faith the more that community of faith changes who I am. [And] the more it changes who I am the more I want to be engaged with it." She expressed heartbreak that more people, especially queer women, aren't able to experience the transformative potential of church communities. "I feel a profound sense of sadness because there's so many people in our community that have been turned off by the hate-mongers [who have] turned them away from these communities that are full of love. I feel a lot of sadness about that. Sometimes, it brings me to tears."

TO CHURCH OR NOT TO CHURCH?

I've heard many pastors and Christian leaders speak about the importance of staying in Christian community. They teach that the Christian life is not meant to be lived in isolation but that we need each other; specifically, we need the church. I've wrestled with this question more than any other since my decision to come out. I've been frustrated with the church, and I've been unable to leave it. Maybe it's because I've had too many positive experiences. Or, maybe I've heard too many warnings about the futility of a "just me and Jesus" approach to faith. Either way, my need to stay involved in community has not subsided with time or with my frustration with the church.

It should be no surprise that churches teach us that we need community. Just like schools will teach that we need an education and gyms will teach that we need to work out. Still, the inherent bias in each of these claims doesn't mean that they are not true. I can't think of many worthwhile endeavors that are best pursued in isolation.

All of the women I interviewed had significant conflict with the church. Whether or not they struggled with internal questions about being right or wrong, they all had to deal with the institution of the Christian church and its many flaws. Some left church completely, some stayed and challenged pastors and other authorities, and some found new, more welcoming communities. Whatever their choice, many resolved this conflict, in part, by reminding themselves that their faith was in God and not in religious leaders or institutions. They found ways to feel connected to God—with or without the church.

My Story: Wrestling with the Church

After returning from my silent retreat, it was clear to me that I needed to come out to people at church. They already knew that I "struggled with unwanted same-sex attractions," but I didn't consider that phrase the same as coming out. To me, coming out meant identifying as lesbian and sharing my belief that there was nothing wrong with same-gender relationships.

My two closest friends at church happened to be on staff. Both of them listened to me, heard my process of hearing from God, and agreed that it seemed as if this was God speaking. They knew me well enough to know how deeply unhappy I'd been. My coming out challenged them to rethink their interpretation of the Bible and their beliefs about homosexuality. I was surprised by how many of my closest friends were fully supportive. Some had expressed a theological objection to same-sex relationships in the past. Others had already held an affirming theology but never pushed their views on me because they'd wanted to remain supportive of my decisions and my own sense of what God was calling me to do. I felt lucky to be surrounded by people who trusted my experience and judgment.

Despite the strong support of my closest friends, the church was still divided in their thinking about LGBTQ issues. The senior pastors, Bill and Debbie, let me know that they would be reconsidering my leadership in the church. They had me over for dinner to try to understand the change in my beliefs. I told them how I felt God had been speaking to me about "a new door" that was being opened and that I had not been happy or healthy denying my sexual orientation. They listened and then explained that they felt pressure from all different angles and that it would be difficult for them to make a decision about my ongoing leadership. They said that the decision would take some time. Then, we ended the night.

After that, debates between staff went on behind closed doors. Most of the congregation was completely unaware of the conflict. The question at hand was whether or not I should be allowed to stay in a leadership position with the recovery group. Bill and Debbie felt that allowing me to lead would be condoning homosexuality, and therefore condoning sin. My friends who were on staff risked their jobs as they argued for me to stay, stating that it was possible that God was leading me to come out as lesbian. They argued that if homosexual relationships are "sin," then they are more like gluttony and less like adultery (meaning they should not exclude people from leadership). The pastors took nine months to discuss, read outside material, pray, and eventually decide whether or not they'd allow me to continue leading in the recovery group.

Bill and Debbie asked to speak with me again to communicate their decision. Bill said that they believe that God's plan is clearly for a man and woman to be together. They explained that they could not support my decision to come out, but it didn't make sense to tear the church apart by removing me from the recovery group. He emphasized that this was a special situation and that I would no longer be allowed to teach, preach, or lead a small group—things I'd done well in the past.

During this conversation, Debbie stayed painfully silent. She had invested a lot of time in me, developing my leadership skills. She wanted me to find "healing" and seemed saddened and disappointed. We'd gotten very close when we were meeting together every week. I shared intimate details of my life with her as we worked through the book *Pursuing Sexual Wholeness*[2] together. She sat with me as I cried many times. She knew how painful it had been for me to try to follow the church's teaching. I hoped she would see that coming out was a good thing. Instead, Bill did all the talking. She was hiding, and I was hurt.

This conversation was frustrating. I was mad that I would not be allowed to be in a leadership position, mad that they didn't trust my sense of God's will in my life, and mad that they saw me as a threat to the church rather than an asset. During the following year, I debated whether or not I should leave the church. The first reason I stayed was that I refused to duck away in secret. I wanted others to know that I had nothing to hide. As time went on I liked to tell myself that I was staying in order to push for change from the inside out, and that was certainly part of it. The greater truth was that I needed them. I had lost so much; I didn't want to lose my church as well. They had supported me through career failure, foreclosure, depression, self-harm, and the ups and downs of daily life for the past six years. They'd prayed with me, fasted with me, invested in me as a leader, and became a second family to me. I loved them.

The church never did split. Thankfully, my friends kept their jobs and the community stayed together. After decisions were made about me, the staff needed time to set aside their differences and work on rebuilding their relationships. They called for a period of time when they wouldn't speak publically about any issues related to homosexuality. For me, the conflict simmered and lingered in awkward silences and overly nice small talk. My attempts to continue discussions with Bill and Debbie were ignored or met with veiled anger. The more I felt silenced, the more I wanted to push back. The more I pushed back the more I made things hard for my friends on staff. This was not my intent. My friends had risked their jobs and future careers for me and my cause. I believed in what I was doing there, but it

2. Comiskey, *Pursuing Sexual Wholeness*.

seemed to be costing them more than it was costing me. When the conflict started to hurt our friendships, the cost of staying in the church became too much.

Three years after coming out, in my final year of grad school, I asked myself, "Why am I working so hard to stay connected to this church when it is causing me so much pain and frustration?" I'd seen some movement towards a more inclusive community, but we'd come to a standstill. After eight years in the church that I loved, I left. I left with both relief and sadness. I knew in my heart that it was the right decision for me, and yet I was heartbroken that I didn't have a place there anymore.

I'm still heartbroken.

Despite this loss, since coming out I've never had to go without an affirming faith community. Just as it was clear to me that I needed to leave my Vineyard church, I came across a new community that seemed incredibly promising. They were building a church that was evangelical in style of music and sermons but progressive in theology and affirming of LGBTQ people. One of the pastors was a young gay man just out of the local Baptist seminary. I loved their vision, but the actual fleshing out of relationships and leadership did not include the collaboration I was hoping to find. Soon the leadership of four pastors dropped down to just one. Instead of fighting for acceptance and support of my leadership, I found myself fighting for more voices to be heard in creating this promising community. I eventually decided that I wanted to stop fighting.

Once again, just as it was time to leave, I became aware of a new community that gave me hope for belonging. I learned of a Lutheran church that was filled with hipster-artists who didn't take themselves too seriously and brought in beautiful original music for the liturgy. It was a different style from what I was used to, but it was a place that I didn't have to fight. I hope I will find belonging there for a long time to come.

For years before coming out, I'd made a morning practice of reading from a book of daily prayers. Every day, the opening prayer is taken from Psalm 27:4. It reads:

> One thing I asked of the Lord
> that will I seek after:
> to live in the house of the Lord
> all the days of my life,
> to behold the beauty of the Lord,
> and to inquire in his temple. (NRSV)

This prayer took on new meaning for me after coming out at church. In the midst of the conflict with pastors of my Vineyard church, I took comfort in asking God that I would always have a place in the church. It grounded me in my faith to make that a daily commitment, saying, "I will seek" a community of people who follow Jesus, and I will ask God to provide it for "all the days of my life." I've worried that there is no place for me, but so far this has not been true. I've always had a church home since coming out and for this I've been grateful.

Not all of my participants stayed involved in organized religion, but nearly all spoke about finding other affirming believers as they worked out their faith questions. Recognizing their need for support, they sought others who could model a life of faith that was more inclusive than they'd known.

Those who found affirming communities spoke very positively of their experiences within them. Their biggest frustration was that their communities couldn't attract more queer women. They wanted more of their friends to experience what they had found to be meaningful. Laurie (a minister in the United Church of Christ) and Gretchen (who attends a Lutheran Church) were deeply committed to their churches at the time of the interviews, and both wished they knew how to effectively reach out to others who'd been harmed by the church. Jacqueline spoke at length about her relationship with the church and the challenges she faced in finding a lasting church home.

JACQUELINE: "YOU NEVER FIND EVERYTHING YOU WANT IN A CHURCH"

Jacqueline described her process of coming to terms with the many flaws of the Catholic Church and determined that she could either choose to take part in it or not. She and her daughter, Amy, went through confirmation together, and Jacqueline questioned if she should commit to a church that wasn't affirming.

> I remember feeling like joining the church was a move out of adolescence because confirmation is the adolescent rite of passage. I had this adolescent relationship with the church, where it was like, "Okay, I'll go, but I'm not really gonna join because the Catholic Church is so screwed up." I remember joining the church, and that became for me a way of saying, "I have to grow up and say, 'Guess

what? The church isn't perfect." I'm gonna decide as an adult to have this relationship with an imperfect institution." It's funny. [Joining my church] ended my early childhood faith experience.

Years later, she and Amy started attending the Baptist church. They both wanted a racially diverse church and both came from very different church cultures. Jacqueline never felt fully at home at the Baptist church, saying, "You never find everything you want in a church." She described the pros and cons of different options available to her. "[The congregational church] is a good church in a lot of ways, but it is just not a fit for me. When I was in seminary I sang in a gospel choir, and, like I said, I grew up in this interracial—more predominantly black—church, so having an interracial faith experience means a lot to me." Jacqueline was well aware that inter-racial *and* affirming churches are hard to come by.

Jacqueline seemed surprised by how it felt to attend Amy's new church, which was not fully affirming but seemed to be moving in that direction. "It feels really moving to me. In some ways it feels more moving than being in a church that is already 100 percent gay affirming because it feels like [the pastor] is doing such important work." She continued, "He is a man of God. And he's a good preacher. I can go there. I get great music, and I get some really good preaching that gives me food for thought and has made me think about things in my life. So that's good, that's all good. And it means a lot to me—(begins to cry). I'm emotional again, gosh—to be able to have a church home with Amy. We used to go to [Catholic Church] together and that was really special to me. That meant a lot."

REASONS FOR COMING OUT

Reconciling faith and sexuality for my participants was often a long process, full of uncertainty and doubt, but it consistently led to a richer faith life and a sense of wholeness. Participants found a personal faith that had survived the fire and emerged as something strong and beautiful. Finding an integrated life involved both developing an affirming belief system and developing relationships where they no longer had to hide or be judged. Coming out to others allowed these women to articulate and stand up for what they knew to be true of them and of God. They spoke with conviction and held their heads high. Consequences were often harsh, but rarely permanent.

When I asked Jacqueline what led her to come out at church, she joked, "There was this beautiful butch woman there, what else was I gonna do?" The others had a few more reservations. Some did not get a choice in the matter and were outed before they were ready. Some are still not fully out in all of their social circles. Some were slow and cautious about coming out at church, work, or with family; others took pride in being as out as they possibly could, challenging stereotypes and advocating for change. Reasons for telling others varied, but all the reasons were connected to a need for personal health and support.

Coming Out for Emotional Wholeness

Coming out is an act of self-advocacy, speaking what is true of oneself despite pressure to conform. Participants came out to others because keeping themselves hidden was painful. They felt isolated from loved ones and unhappy with themselves for the dishonesty it took to stay in the closet. Participants decided to come out because they believed it could lead to personal health. They used terms like "wholeness," "congruency," "integrity," "authenticity," and "connectedness" to describe their reasons for coming out to others.

Seeing the unhealthy patterns of my own life and the lives of other women in my situation was the most influential factor in challenging my beliefs about what was okay for me and what wasn't. I had a strong belief that following God is good for us, that following Jesus is the best life possible, but I was not living it. I was living a pattern of push and pull—longing and fearful avoidance. As I looked ahead, I saw a life full of no-win relationships. Seeing these patterns of painful relationships repeat themselves in my life made me question what I could do differently. Seeing my friends repeat the same patterns that kept them miserable made me ask, "What are we doing? Is this really what God requires?"

One ray of hope in the LGBTQ community is that the popular "It Gets Better" campaign seems to be true on a measurable level—life does seem to get better for LGBTQ people as they get older. In a study comparing gay and straight men with mental health diagnoses, they found that gay men had a significant reduction in depression, suicidality, anxiety, anger, shame, and other symptoms as they got older. Straight men only experienced a reduction in anger; they did not improve in other areas with age.[3] Once

3. Bybee et al., "Are Gay Men in Worse Mental Health?," 149–50.

again, the same study does not exist for women, but I suspect the results would be similar. When LGBTQ people are given enough time to create their own supportive communities and time to challenge negative societal messages about them, they overcome stigma and grow into happier and healthier individuals.

Coming Out to Gain Support

Connected to the need for emotional health is the need for supportive relationships. Loving relationships are our most basic human need; without them we wither away into fear, bitterness, or despair. Before coming out to people who are likely to reject us, most LGBTQ individuals seek out allies or others within the queer community who can provide the support they need. Kimberly would sneak out of her mother's house to find support at District 202; Laurie sought out affirming churches before graduating from Bible college; Hannah joined campus Alliance; Renae found mentors; and Ericka came out to friends. All of these resources are crucial for young people who are queer or questioning. Still, as Maureen put it, "Friends can only give you so much." She needed her family.

After coming out myself, my attempts to meet other queer women were not initially successful. The local gay church consisted of mostly men, and I couldn't imagine trying to make friends in a bar, so I did the stereotypical lesbian networking move and joined a softball team. I met a few great people there, but it was not the warm welcome into the lesbian community that I was hoping it would be. After watching my teammates narrowly escape a bar fight, I started looking for other ways to meet people.

In time, I met a very solid group of queer women friends. They make good-natured fun of me and my faith by apologizing to me after swearing and laughing at the silliness of wasting a leisurely Sunday morning at church. They also have shown respect for my attempts to push for inclusion in my church and the greater Christian community.

For a long time I felt torn between two worlds, but more and more I have been able to truly be myself like never before. Now, I can be me among lesbians and me among Christians, and me among social workers, family, and friends. This feels amazing. Being able to give up the need to fit in among different groups of people was liberating. Now, I don't feel torn at all. My world includes friends from my old church, friends from my new church, and friends who would never be caught dead in a church. I love that I have developed close relationships with people from all different walks of life and that I can be myself with them all.

In essence, many queer people come out because it is too painful not to. We come out because an integrated, fulfilling, and honest life is possible on the other side of the closet door. Authentic relationships, emotional support, and freedom to be ourselves are all possible when we are able to find healthy, affirming environments.

10

Reclamation: The Abundant Life

FINDING THE GOOD NEWS

JESUS SAID, "I CAME that they may have life, and have it abundantly."[1] This Scripture has been ingrained in me since I was eighteen and attending my first meetings of my campus Christian group. The staff members emphasized the message that following Jesus leads to "the good life" and that the gospel is, indeed, good news. I've held on to the conviction that God wants our lives to be fulfilling, healthy, whole, and rewarding. This is not at all a life without pain, or a life of getting everything we want, but a life that is more fully human than how we used to live. It's a life that calls us to love more, risk more, give more, and to let go of fear, anger, and narcissistic self-interest. I wholeheartedly believe that following Jesus leads to an abundant life. Sadly, religion can really mess things up.

The stories we've heard from women so far speak to the way that religion has messed things up for them, leading to shame, depression, rejection, loss, and even violence and homelessness. Despite the pain that is evident in each woman's life, their stories also reveal the work of God, as they were able to find ways to be their whole selves: open to relationships that they find satisfying *and* following Jesus as best they could. They described their current lives in terms like "healthy," "whole," "authentic," "happy," and "comfortable" with themselves. They also felt, "jaded," "lonely,"

1. John 10:10 NRSV.

127

or "mad" about the ways certain Christians have treated them and other queer people. They all saw God as the one who offers full acceptance and love, no matter what the church may do.

This was the best news I discovered in my research: whether or not the church fully accepts us, God is still at work in our lives and in the world. Rejection from the church could not keep God from revealing him or herself to us. There is great sadness and loss in being left out of a life-giving community, but it does not keep us from experiencing a loving God. The church does not hold that kind of power. These women encountered God in church, but also in the wilderness, in the Bible, in their own spiritual practices, and in other believers. They still felt the transforming power of the love of God.

The belief that following God is good for us is what led me to rethink my theology and to come out as lesbian and Christian. Scripture suggests that following God leads to love, joy, peace, patience, kindness, generosity, faithfulness, gentleness, and self-control.[2] These are the fruits of the Spirit—evidence of the Spirit's work in our lives. The stories I gathered were filled with evidence of the Spirit's work. Participants often described their current faith as more meaningful than it had ever been before. They gained a sense of their own honesty, integrity, health, and freedom as a result of coming out and finding safe places. They began to see God as more loving and accepting than they had known God to be in the past.

Renae described her current faith, saying, "It's the healthiest it's ever been because I am able to be honest with myself, honest with others." This kind of honesty is essential for personal and spiritual growth. Others showed a similar progression into self-acceptance and a rich spiritual life.

Integrating faith and sexuality was often associated with the development of a more positive self-image and a more positive image of God, two things that tend to be very connected.[3] The progression of participants' image of God reflects growth in their personal and emotional health. Most of the participants reported that their beliefs about God moved from judgmental or rule-bound to loving and accepting. Maureen explained, "I used to think God was this being that punished. That He was like the police; if you did something wrong, you get in trouble." Now, she sees things differently. "God is more like [a] helping hand to me now, rather than an authoritative figure. . . . Being gay and coming out to my family and to Sara's

2. Gal. 5:22–23 NRSV.

3. Benson and Spilka, "God Image as a Function of Self-Esteem," 297–310.

family—because I had to come out twice—did change my view on God. It made me think that God was more of a loving creature then a disapproving one."

A few participants indicated that their belief in God had not changed. For each of them, God was and had always been very loving and accepting. This was true of Anita. She experienced transformation, not in her view of God but in her view of herself. "Before, I felt very shamed, very shameful of who I was and who I loved. I've come to the opinion [that]—no matter what—I know God still loves me, even if everybody else has a problem with who I am and what I'm doing. I know that God just wrapped His arms around me and comforted me and showed me mercy and grace."

What I found most striking about the stories that came out of my research was the deeply profound spiritual experiences and current faith of my participants. Perhaps I, too, bought into stereotypes that queer people are not interested in spiritual matters or that they hold an anything goes, fluffy, feel-good spirituality. Maybe I expected more people to be jaded and bitter. Whatever my underlying misconceptions may have been, I was surprised by the depth of wisdom, faith, and commitment these women revealed. They wanted to show grace and love to those who harmed them, share a message of loving-acceptance with other queer people, and learn from others along the way. I was baffled to so easily find faith among those cast out of the church. Participants spoke of transformation from shame and hiding to freedom, self-acceptance, and love. Despite their many painful experiences and ongoing frustrations with Christians, they have known the goodness of God in the land of the living, and they were grateful.

CALLING AND ADVOCACY

In several interviews, participants spoke about a sense of calling or mission. This calling may have been present early on in life, but was often vague and out of reach. Over time, this calling became clear and opportunities arose to live out what they felt called to do. This was especially true of Lawrence (whose story is described in the next chapter) and Laurie, who both felt called into professional ministry. Jacqueline felt called to be engaged in the world, fighting against injustice and working towards equality. Others spoke of calling as a sense of purpose that had been made clear to them, or as something common to every Christian. Often, this calling involved carrying a message of acceptance and love to the queer community.

Strangely, I felt called to the LGBTQ community years before I accepted same-gender relationships. I felt that the church's focus on the sin of gay people was unfounded and their treatment of LGBTQ people was, often, abusive. I knew that I was supposed to bring a message of God's love, but I didn't know how. I knew that it was not a message that would be very well received as long as I believed that it was wrong to pursue same-gender relationships. Still, my heart was broken over how Christians have treated the gay community. I felt called to challenge the church to love people with whom they disagree, to stop making gay people the butt of their jokes, and to consider how differently they treat people whose sins include divorce, greed, and gluttony.

I knew that I wasn't just called to bring a message to my church but that I was called to LGBTQ people. This calling felt impossible. I had no message of good news to offer. "Come, live a life of celibacy!" was not a message I wanted to share. Christianity was a hard truth to me; encouraging people to follow Jesus and give up any chance of finding loving relationships did not seem like a reasonable calling or "good news." Not until I was able to see that God was also calling me to come out as a lesbian Christian, did I see a path laid out before me. Then I could see my own calling to take part in a movement of Jesus followers who were proclaiming the love of God for all people.

The sense of calling that participants experienced and the clear direction they heard from God are reminiscent of the story of the good shepherd and the sheep who know his voice. Jesus taught, "My sheep listen to my voice; I know them, and they follow me." This was a very real experience for my participants. They had heard the voice of God and responded faithfully. Listening to the call of God brought them joy and a sense of purpose.

WHY KEEP FAITH?

The process of integrating the various pieces of oneself takes time and effort for both gay and straight people alike. It becomes far more difficult when these pieces seem to be in conflict with one another. Because plenty of people have suggested that organized religion causes more harm than good, one question I asked my participants, "What made you hold on to your faith?" It was important for me to ask this question of others, to see what made them either hold on to their beliefs or return to their beliefs after a period of stepping away and what value they saw in their faith practices.

Participants often held on to faith because of meaningful spiritual experiences in their past and the desire to make a future that centered on following God. Some felt called to bring a message of acceptance to others, and some were still wrestling with their own questions.

It's interesting to me how many women imagined a life without faith as being "empty," "miserable," "angry," and "not whole." Some couldn't imagine their lives without trusting in God. They saw faith as something that could bring fulfillment, something more powerful or meaningful than living for themselves, something that could offer hope and solace and help them to become better people.

Some held onto faith because of memories of God reaching out to them, like Ericka in the wilderness of Montana when she heard God say, "You are not a mistake." Some, like Amy, lived without God for years and looked back at that time as empty and meaningless. Some, like Maureen, saw God as the bearer of hope and unconditional love in a world full of pain and injustice. Renae knew that she needed faith (and community) for her own growth in becoming the person she wanted to be. These are the beautiful things a life of faith has to offer, and these things were still available to the women I interviewed. They benefitted from their faith in God, and they found good news in the gospel.

HOPE FOR CHANGE IN FAMILIES

Most of the women I interviewed spoke about how they witnessed improvements in their families over time. While the initial response to their coming out was often painful—with parental messages of disapproval or rejection—parents typically took steps towards acceptance and love. Some parents had a complete turnaround in their beliefs, like Ericka's mother who went from kicking Ericka out of the home to expressing full support of whomever she chose to date. Maureen's in-laws attended her and Sara's wedding, said "I love you" often, and expressed full support after objecting to Maureen and Sara's relationship and quoting Scripture at them. Some parents took smaller steps towards understanding their daughter and maintaining a relationship. Renae's mother still does not approve, but now they have a "surface"-level relationship in which they can still be involved in each other's lives (which was not the case for several years). Parents may need time to grieve the dreams they had for their child; they may need to gather accurate information about LGBTQ people;[4] and they may need to wrestle with their own religious beliefs. All these things can bring about an improved relationship if all parties are willing.

I'm so grateful for the improved relationship I have with my parents. They've never said, "I told you so," or "It took you long enough" to come out. Instead, they offered an apology for not understanding the importance that my faith had in my life. After a decade of distance and conflict, we finally have a relationship of vulnerability and trust. We enjoy each other's company, and the awkwardness and hurt that were once there are gone. They crack me up every time I see them, and they always let me know that I'm loved.

4. LaSala, "Lesbians, Gay Men, and Their Parents," 72.

11

Reclamation: Transformation

EACH STORY I GATHERED was a story of transformation. Each woman was transformed by encountering God in very real ways, whether by catching the mission of social-justice-oriented faith, by encountering God in the wilderness, by finding a life-giving community, or by studying scriptures in a new light; all had life-altering spiritual experiences. Some stories were more dramatic than others, but each spoke to the ways in which following God has improved their lives. Many also spoke of being transformed by self-acceptance—especially those who had taken in more negative beliefs about their orientation. They rejected the "meta-narrative" that said they were sinful or unchristian, and developed a new life story that revealed their strength, courage, faithfulness, and integrity. They found abundant living after knowing shame and despair.

LAWRENCE: "I FEEL UNBOUND."

No story spoke more profoundly about transformation than did Lawrence's. I met Lawrence at the same PFLAG meeting that I met Gretchen. He was also on the faith panel, along with a lesbian rabbi, a gay Episcopal priest, and me. Lawrence identifies as a female-to-male transgender man. When we met for the interview, he was thirty-two years old and had completed his transition to male. He is African American and grew up in a Baptist church that was quite hostile to LGBTQ people.

The term transgender is "an umbrella term that refers to people who live differently than the gender presentation and roles expected of them by society."[1] For Lawrence, it means he was born female but never felt like that gender fit him. He lived as Lateasha until he was twenty-eight when he began his transition. He has undergone surgery and receives hormone treatments to complete the physical transition to male. When I met him, I assumed he was a gay man (he is actually attracted to both men and women) and was surprised to learn that he was not born male.

Lawrence's story is inherently different than my other participants. I was hesitant to ask him to take part in this project because this book is about queer women, and I did not want to offend him. Still, I found his story so compelling that I thought I'd ask his opinion about being included. He assured me that I did not offend him. He pointed out that he did live as female until he was twenty-eight and may have an important perspective to include since he has experienced life in both genders.

I was most impressed by how Lawrence had been transformed—not from female to male, but from depressed to joyful, suicidal to full of hope. His transition seemed to save his life. And, his faith sustained him through it all. He is now a minister with the United Church of Christ, a board member of PFLAG, and a business owner selling products for transgender people.

Lawrence spoke with pride about his spiritual heritage:

> I grew up in the church; my family is filled with missionaries and preachers and evangelists. My parents were married in the church I grew up in, and my grandma was one of the founding members. I was Southern Baptist and grew up in a tradition [where] you showed your commitment by baptism. Not infant baptism—believer's baptism. It's funny that it's called believer's baptism because it insinuates that you get to a point where you believe, and now you're making this decision to be baptized. But I was told, "You're going to get baptized." There was never a choice. So I was baptized at six. And four years later I felt like it was time for me to make [my own] decision to become baptized because I felt called; so I was baptized a second time. Then, when I was ordained, I was baptized a third time. So I've been baptized a lot! But that explains my journey because everything was church. I loved church; I loved that that was where I received community. I had a really abusive home life, and school life was tragic and not fun either, so church was

1. NCTE, "Teaching Transgender," 18.

the place that I went to for everything. And it was a very positive experience for me until high school.

Lawrence then laughed, indicating that the positive experiences at church came to an abrupt end.

Lawrence had to come out several times, first as lesbian or queer, and then later as transgender. He explained to me that when referring to him prior to the transition, the word "she" is appropriate for ease of understanding, though present tense he prefers "he." For this reason I use different pronouns at different times for him. Lawrence described a bit about what it was like for him growing up. "I just thought I was a boy until I hit puberty and everybody started telling me that I was a girl, and it was like, 'Oh crap, really? Well then I better become a girl.' That's literally what I thought. I thought, 'I'd better *become* a girl.' So I started dressing really feminine; I did modeling for a while, dance class. I was a gymnast and everything really feminine. I thought that it would one day just take, and it never did." Lawrence laughed and added again, "It never did."

As a child, Lateasha found it helpful to have her mom buy her boxer shorts, or wear other male clothing. Lawrence said, "I have pictures from my earliest birthday party where she let me wear a tie because I wanted to." He added, "For Halloween I'd dress up as a boy, but in my other public everyday life I was very feminine." Lateasha worked hard at living up to the expectations of others. "I tried really hard to do those things, and for three or four years before high school I did a pretty good job. I was still a tomboy, but it was okay. Once I hit high school it was like, 'Maybe I'm just a lesbian; that makes total sense.' I started to date girls. I was still dating guys, but I felt like that was a name, like that was something to define what was happening."

Lateasha knew that identifying as lesbian was not acceptable in her church, so she started to compartmentalize.

> I became closeted at church but out everywhere else. (Laughs.) That was proving to not be enough either. I didn't identify as a lesbian. I [had] thought that was the word, and it didn't fit because I still didn't identify as a woman. I knew I was attracted to women, and I knew that I was also attracted to men, but the word lesbian wasn't enough. Then I started to claim the word bisexual, and then I thought that doesn't fit either because I still don't identify as a woman. I didn't know I could identify as a man, so I just thought that I was queer. At about fifteen that's when I said I'm queer.

He explained, "I still identify as queer." He laughed and added, "But with more information."

Church was an integral part of Lateasha's life, but she knew that it was not a place that she could be her true self. "I felt like I was living two lives. I couldn't bring all of myself to such a deep experience, and I felt like I was missing something. I couldn't be all of myself. I had to pretend and hold back and be on guard all the time. How can you have a life-changing spiritual experience if there is a part of your spirit that you can't even embrace? That was crushing. It started to become a negative experience, going to church."

Lateasha started feeling distanced from others at church and began growing uncomfortable with the inconsistencies she noticed between the stated values of church members and their actions. "I felt like I was a part of it but still on the outside because, although the spiritual part of it was amazing and nurturing and it fed my soul, there was the religious part of it." The religious part is what Lawrence identified as rituals and prayers that professed values that the church did not live up to, mainly, treating others with love and respect.

> I would see people get ridiculed and made fun of. My pastor would do his annual sermon on why gay people are going to hell. He would get up there and he would imitate gay people, and he would walk with his hand on his hips and switch around the pulpit. It was awful. I could look around the congregation and see people just sinking inside of themselves, lowering their heads in shame. As a kid watching this, I couldn't name what was happening, but I knew that whatever he was talking about [was] making them feel negative. And it was making me feel negative, and I didn't know why. I remember thinking 'That's not God.'

Lateasha saw her pastor acting this way and thought, "You making fun of someone, this is why I hate going to school." When she saw the same mocking from the pulpit, she said, "It started to put a wedge between me and the church. I started to realize at about thirteen or fourteen that something's not right here. Not not right with me, but something's not right *here*."

Despite recognizing problems with the church and inconsistencies in their beliefs and behavior, Lateasha still wrestled with her own beliefs. "On one hand, I was hearing that God hated me and anybody like me, but on the other hand, I felt that was a lie and that God did love me, because I felt it." For a while, she tried to argue with others without coming out to them, with little success. Lawrence added, "I think the missing piece would've been, 'I'm queer and I feel the love of God every day, so you're wrong!' But instead [it] became a Scripture argument and that never wins."

Several events occurred that made it clear to Lateasha that her church was no longer safe. First, she knew of a neighbor and church member who was threatened and physically assaulted by other members of the church after coming out. After that, hearing another sermon that ridiculed gay people made the decision final. Lawrence remembered thinking, "Either God didn't affirm me and I was wrong, or they were wrong and God did affirm me; but I knew that I couldn't be at church."

Despite this clear path, leaving her community was painful. "I felt like my spirit was taken and put in a box and set on a shelf. I struggled for a while after that because I felt such a deep connection to my church, and to lose that—I lost my entire foundation. The next few years were very difficult."

These difficult years included severe depression and multiple suicide attempts. Lawrence said, "From the age of nine to twenty I tried to kill myself probably a dozen times. And the only thing that would've [made a] difference would've been [to hear], 'I love you and you're okay just the way you are.'" Questions about God, sexual and gender identity, and the church's teachings fueled her misery during these years. She asked, "Does God really love me? Because I'm losing everything—my family, my church, my friends—all because. . . . Am I sure I even feel this? Is it identity? Is it orientation?" These questions are what led her to a final suicide attempt. Lateasha wrote a letter before overdosing that went something like this:

> God, if this is not your will, if this is not for me and I'm gonna
> go to hell anyway and you hate me, then just let me die because I
> don't want to live in hell and then die and go to hell. I think that is
> a pointless waste of time. But, if I'm okay exactly the way that I am
> and you love me for everything that I am, then bring me out of this
> to show people. I will dedicate the rest of my life—if this is you, if
> this is who I am and it's okay with you—I will dedicate the rest of
> my life to making sure that everybody knows that.

Lawrence recalled that the first thing Lateasha felt upon waking up in the hospital was surprise to be alive. He said, "That shocked me because that meant that there was some part of me that actually believed all of the crap that my church told me. I woke up and I thought, 'Oh crap, I don't have a plan B.'" Lawrence laughed and added, "But, here we are."

It's hard to imagine anything more miserable than foreseeing a life of suffering with eternal torment at the end of it. It's also hard to imagine Lawrence in such a place of misery. Today, he radiates joy and positive energy. He advocates for change with warmth and optimism. He attributes this change to the loving acceptance he's been able to find in new communities and that he is finally able to live in a body that he loves. His transformation was dramatic, from suicidal to full of hope and joy.

After I heard about the religious blessing that Jacqueline sought out for Marcus and herself, I wondered if Lawrence had wanted some sort of ritual ceremony around his transition. It turns out that he too wanted God's blessing and the support of his faith community. "Right before my gender reassignment surgery, my pastor and some representatives from our conference staff and people from my church and family all got together, and I had an unbinding ceremony—literally taking off my binder, but also figuratively removing that [which] kept me bound as a person that I did not feel aligned with. It was really cool."

I asked how this unbinding has changed things for him.

He replied, "I really feel unbound." He paused as he held back tears. "I feel free. That next day, going into preparation for surgery, I was in this space of releasing. I feel like a lot of the crap, the beating up of my spirit, all of that crap was taken away and I feel lighter. I joke with my friends; I say, 'The longer I'm transitioning the gayer I become because I am so excited now and so happy and filled with so much life; it is amazing!"

Lawrence has been able to carry on a message of hope to others. During his transition, he kept a video blog to share with others around the world. He said, "When I watch some of the earlier videos, I was in so much pain. I was miserable. That makes me sad to watch that and to know that I lived that, but it also makes me happy that I'm no longer in that space."

Before the transition, Lateasha attended Liberty Theological Seminary—the one founded by Jerry Falwell, who was well known for promoting anti-gay views and blaming gay people for AIDS, the 9/11 attacks, and the supposed moral decline of America. I asked Lawrence what on earth led him to go there. He said, "I chose a Baptist seminary because that is how I learned how to read the Bible and interpret things and to analyze things. It's my language—not necessarily my beliefs—if that makes any sense." Choosing the distance learning program at Liberty protected Lateasha from being surrounded by the evangelical culture and allowed her to have the credentials that no pastor she knew could discredit. She held the belief that change in the church would have to come from within. She knew that her own church would be far less likely to listen to outsiders.

> I grew up in a Baptist church that did not affirm who I was. I'm going to a Baptist seminary that did not affirm who I was. At that time, I was a woman who was a minister; that right there was not okay. [It was a] predominantly white school and I was black; that was difficult. There was all kinds of difficult things. I did it because I want to be able to have the credentials to go back into these spaces and be taken as an equal, which I have been able to do now. It's learning how to play that game. I want to have just as much right to sit at this table, and I don't want you to give me any reason why I can't be here because my voice needs to be added to this discussion.

I wondered how these discussions with other pastors have gone for him. "The ministers that were over me as a child are now colleagues of mine, and that's interesting because they don't know who I am. They don't remember me because I am now male. They talk to me differently. But now that I have quote-unquote 'authority,' I'm able to say things to them that I wasn't able to say twenty years ago as a kid."

I was very curious about what it was like for him to encounter these pastors who mocked gay people by prancing around the pulpit and promoting a community of shame and violence. He said, "It's fantastic! I absolutely love it because I was completely powerless as a child, watching them make fun of gay people [and] talk horribly about anybody that's different. Now, as an adult male pastor [who is] on their level with as much education, I'm able to say, 'I am a transgender man and what you're saying is wrong.' Now, instead of the degrading comments, [they say,] 'Well I guess we'll just have to agree to disagree.'"

Clearly the pastors had not changed their minds, but Lawrence was no longer silenced or powerless. Now, he was a well-educated adult who was able to articulate his truth to people who had harmed him. It takes a special kind of strength to go back to the places you've been hurt and to communicate with those who have held power over you. It is clear that he feels compelled to challenge authorities and to bring a message of hope to others. "Another thing that I would love the world to see—I am free now. It's because I've embraced exactly who I am, and I've embraced God in me and it's wonderful. How can I be an abomination to God when I am this free? The meaning of the word 'salvation' is to be whole. I feel whole, I feel free, I feel amazing!" Lawrence doesn't just talk about freedom and joy, but he exudes this positivity in his daily life. I was moved by his story as I heard it at the PFLAG meeting where we first met. Not only that, but I was struck by his positive attitude toward faith communities after such painful experiences.

Lawrence's story is obviously different than mine and different than the stories of the women I interviewed. His story may not fit the mold of my research project, but I wanted to include it because I found it quite remarkable. He was transformed from hopelessness and despair to joy, purpose, and abundance. He barely survived his childhood but has emerged as a generous, hopeful, and inspiring man. I needed to make a place for such a powerful story.

Despite the differences between Lawrence's story and the stories of the others, there are similarities in the ways that nearly all found freedom to be themselves that was not there before. They were thrown into spiritual crises that resulted in significant losses in addition to self-acceptance and deep faith. Most often, my interview participants emerged from their experiences with both sadness or grief and a newfound sense of wholeness. Losses were profound, yet gaining wholeness should not be underappreciated. Without feeling like whole people we cannot feel peace, health, security, or a clear sense of ourselves. Since coming out at my church, I feel a freedom similar to that which Lawrence described. I resonated with his logic, asking myself, "How can this be wrong when it has brought me so much joy, self-acceptance, freedom, and hope?" I love my life! How can this be so wrong? "I feel whole, I feel free, I feel amazing!"

12

Conclusions

SOLA SCRIPTURA WAS ADOPTED as a key concept of the Protestant Reformation. No longer did Christians need to rely on the corrupt institution that was the Catholic Church of that time to tell them what was right. Taking the Bible into their own hands, people were free to seek out truth for themselves in the context of Christian community. History reveals some of the problems with this method of seeking truth. One protest led to another, and the churches have been splitting ever since. I think it is safe to say that in each of these church divisions, both sides have walked away with the conviction that they were interpreting the Bible accurately and that the others got it all wrong.

Letting go of my conviction that the Bible could be an accurate, stand-alone source for determining what is right and good was a little scary. I found myself questioning all I'd been taught and had come to believe about sex, relationships, truth, and what it means to follow Jesus. I feared letting go of my convictions because I wondered, "What now?" Would I transform into a hedonistic, sex-crazed, party animal? (That was probably more fantasy than fear, but, for better or for worse, it did not happen.) I'm still me—cautious and shy and taking myself too seriously. My fear of losing any sense of morality was unfounded. Dating has been fun and awkward and exciting and heartbreaking—all the things that dating should be. It has not led to complete moral relativism or a descent into depravity. It has given me hope again.

My biggest challenge of the past few years has been to figure out how to actively and passionately push for change and inclusion, and to love the people I'm pushing against. I'm not always able do this without reacting in anger. Still, I know that if I fight intolerance with intolerance for another's religious views, then I'm falling short of my own Christian ideals and I might just be a hypocrite. No matter how right we may prove to be in ten, twenty, fifty years, I still want to love the people who fall on the "wrong side of history." I also think that love may be the most convincing response. Love is disarming, bridge-building, and powerful. It changes people. Loving our enemies is the highest and most difficult calling in Christianity. I don't know how to do it, but I feel compelled to try.

One major step in learning to love others well has been forgiving myself for all of my missteps. It's been hard to reconcile the sudden change in my beliefs—how I could live for so long with the conviction that a certain life path is wrong and then turn around and believe wholeheartedly that the same path is right and good. I searched for some way to make sense of the abrupt changes in my beliefs. So many years seemed lost to an unnecessary sacrifice, and yet I couldn't believe that following God to the best of my knowledge and ability was wasted time. The image of the labyrinth became a symbol that helped me make sense of the many turns I'd taken in life. A labyrinth is not a maze in which you can get lost, but a winding path that leads toward center. The image of a labyrinth encourages me that turning around is part of the journey, that we don't find truth without taking in new information, adjusting our path, and pressing on in a new direction. This is the essence of repentance. Seeing my life as a labyrinth allowed me to look back at my old self without judgment, and to acknowledge that I was on the path set before me. I was moving toward Truth even when I seemed to be going the wrong way. The labyrinth reminds me that as I press on in search of what is true and good, I must be willing to turn around.

The labyrinth also helps me to see that sincere Christians who disapprove of same-gender relationships may be searching for their own truth too. Perhaps we can both be moving towards truth even as we walk in opposite directions. Despite my anger, and how valid I feel it may be, I still want to treat people who disagree with love and kindness. I know that my own views shifted rather quickly, and I remember how bad it felt when others thought my beliefs were ignorant or judgmental. I want to live in such a way that if I ever were to run into a former version of myself, I would be kind. Easier said than done, perhaps, but I can trust that the Spirit is with me, guiding and helping me to find what I need for my faith to survive.

Listening to the spiritual journeys of other queer women has helped me to forgive myself for years that seemed wasted on needless sacrifice and faulty convictions. I can now see that a decade of my life was not wasted by believing it was wrong to love other women, but that I was following God to the best of my ability (which is never a waste). Forgiving myself allows me to extend understanding and forgiveness to others. Many of my participants offered love and forgiveness to loved ones after experiencing more hardship than I've known. Their stories have the familiar theme of God at work, restoring broken relationships and bringing wholeness and blessings. These are the same stories I've heard since I first encountered Jesus: testimonies of people being reconciled to God and to others. They are stories of healing and hope and transformation; stories of the redeemed.

It is my hope that more and more faith communities will adopt fully inclusive and welcoming policies and cultures. There are many resources available for those who need biblical and theological arguments for inclusion. I've always been more moved by story. As it turns out, the Bible is filled with stories pointing toward full inclusion. In the book of Acts, the followers of Jesus did not want to allow gentile believers into their fellowship. Jewish law was clear that Jews were not to associate with gentiles. Peter saw a vision of animals that were, by law, unclean. Peter heard God say, "Kill and eat." When Peter protested, God said, "Do not call anything unclean that I have made clean." It was only after Peter witnessed the Holy Spirit among the gentiles that he set aside the law and tradition in favor of a new way that included those who were once cast out. Peter then explained to the other Jews, "If God gave them the same gift he gave us who believed in the Lord Jesus Christ, who was I to think that I could stand in God's way?" (Acts 11:17 NIV). Early Christians witnessed the work of God among the gentiles and followed the Spirit instead of the law and tradition.

It may be difficult to trust that the Spirit can guide us. The Spirit is not concrete. It cannot be read, referenced, memorized, highlighted, or put in our back pocket. Despite this elusiveness, Jesus referred to the Spirit as *the one* who "will guide you into all truth." Believing that the Bible holds truth and the Spirit holds *the whole truth* is the only way I see for evangelical churches to move forward. I believe we can trust the Spirit to reveal her work in our lives when we follow Jesus.

I see the Spirit's work in the lives of each person I interviewed. They had horrible experiences in the name of God, and yet they still felt called, heard God's voice, responded to an internal sense of emptiness, and searched for truth. Their lives got better as they followed God's voice. Their lives got better as they grew more honest, more authentic, more willing to challenge spiritual authorities, and more willing to stand firm in their convictions. Their hearts broke over the loss of relationships, communities, and family support. They spoke of anger and forgiveness, and loved people through their own processes of acceptance. The health and happiness in my current life is the most convincing bit of evidence that I am still within God's will. Despite grieving the loss of friends and churches, I am happier than I've ever been. I feel comfortable in my own skin and hopeful about my future. Interestingly, I've grown more confident in all areas of my life. I attribute this to finally being able to trust myself and my perception of the world. This has been incredibly liberating. For the first time in my life, I find myself saying too much! I've become known as someone who speaks her mind. I like this about me. I am no longer silent out of fear.

I still mourn the loss of my old church and I pout to my old friends that I don't see enough of them. I still carry too much anxiety for my poor muscles to fully relax and I still twitch from time to time. Sadly, not all of my problems have been magically solved. Still, I love my life and the direction it is going. I feel good about the person I am today. My faith is no longer a hard truth or a bitter pill to swallow but a source of inspiration, wonder and curiosity, meaning and purpose. This project has been my joy-filled obsession and I'm honored to finally be living out my calling, proclaiming the good news of God's incredible love, available to all. This is good news I'm willing to share.

Bibliography

American Psychological Association. *Appropriate Therapeutic Responses to Sexual Orientation.* Washington, DC: American Psychological Association, 2009.

Avery, Alison, Justin Chase, Linda Johansson, Samantha Litvak, Darrel Montero, and Michael Wydra. "America's Changing Attitudes toward Homosexuality, Civil Unions, and Same-Gender Marriage: 1977–2004." *Social Work* 52 (2007) 71–79.

Balsam, Kimberly, Theodore Beauchaine, Ruth Mickey, and Esther Rothblum. "Mental Health of Lesbian, Gay, Bisexual, and Heterosexual Siblings: Effects of Gender, Sexual Orientation, and Family." *Journal of Abnormal Psychology* 114 (2005) 471–76.

Benson, Peter, and Bernard Spilka, "God Image as a Function of Self-Esteem and Locus of Control." *Journal for the Scientific Study of Religion* 12 (1973).

Bradshaw, Matt, and Christopher G. Ellison. "Financial Hardship and Psychological Distress: Exploring the Buffering Effects of Religion." *Social Science & Medicine* 71 (2010) 196–204.

Bybee, Jane A., Eric L. Sullivan, Erich Zielonka, and Elizabeth Moes. "Are Gay Men in Worse Mental Health than Heterosexual Men? The Role of Age, Shame and Guilt, and Coming-out." *Journal of Adult Development* 16 (2009) 144–54.

Carey, Benedict. "Psychiatry Giant Sorry for Backing Gay 'Cure.'" *New York Times,* May 18, 2012, A1.

Comiskey, Andrew. *Pursuing Sexual Wholeness Workbook.* Kansas City, MO: Charisma House, 1989.

Davis, Tamara S., Susan Saltzburg, and Chris Locke. "Supporting the Emotional and Psychological Well Being of Sexual Minority Youth: Youth Ideas for Action." *Children and Youth Services Review* 31 (2009) 1030–41.

Deaton, Angus. "Aging, Religion and Health." NBER Working Paper No. w15271 (2009). Online: http://www.nber.org/papers/w15271.pdf

Editorial Board. "Banning a Pseudo-Therapy." *New York Times,* September 8, 2013, SR10.

Farley, Yvonne R. "Making the Connection: Spirituality, Trauma, and Resiliency." *Journal of Religion & Spirituality* 26 (2007) 1–15.

Foderaro, Lisa. "Private Moment Made Public, Then a Fatal Jump." *New York Times,* September 30, 2010, A1.

James Fowler, *Stages of Faith: The Psychology of Human Development and the Quest for Meaning.* New York: Harper One, 1981.

Friedman, Mark, Michael Marshal, Thomas Guadamuz, Chongyi Wei, Carolyn Wong, Elizabeth Saewyc, and Ron Stall. "Disparities in Childhood Sexual Abuse, Parental

Physical Abuse, and Peer Victimization among Sexual Minority and Sexual Nonminority Individuals." *American Journal of Public Health* 101 (2011) 1481–94.

Garcia, Michelle. "'It's All Our Fault!' 10 Disasters the Gays Supposedly Caused," *The Advocate*, October 31, 2012. Online: http://www.advocate.com/politics/2012/10/31/10-disasters-gays-were-blamed-causing?page=full.

Greene, R. *Resiliency: An Integrated Approach to Practice, Policy, and Research.* Washington, DC: NASW Press, 2002.

Hawkins, Beth. "MN Marriage-amendment Messaging Takes Page from CA's Prop 8 Campaign." *MinnPost*, April 5, 2012, line 40–42. Online: http://www.minnpost.com/politics-policy/2012/04/mn-marriage-amendment-messaging-takes-page-cas-prop-8-campaign.

Hatzenbuehler, Mark L. "The Social Environment and Suicide Attempts in Lesbian, Gay, and Bisexual Youth." *Pediatrics* 127 (2011) 896–903.

Ison, Daniel, Susan Saltzburg, and Sarah Bledsoe. "A Nietzschean Perspective on Church Affiliation and Self-esteem among Same-sex Attracted Members of the Mormon Church." *Journal of Progressive Human Services* 21 (2010) 136–53.

Just the Facts Coalition. *Just the Facts about Sexual Orientation and Youth: A Primer for Principals, Educators, and School Personnel.* Washington, DC: American Psychological Association, 2008.

Kennedy, Tony. "Marcus Bachmann Says His Clinic Is Not Anti-gay." *Star Tribune*, July 15, 2011. Online: http://www.startribune.com/politics/statelocal/125610083.html.

Kimball, Dan. *They Like Jesus But Not the Church: Insights from Emerging Generations.* Grand Rapids: Zondervan, 2007.

LaSala, Michael. "Lesbians, Gay Men, and Their Parents: Family Therapy for the Coming-Out Crisis." *Family Process* 39 (Spring 2000) 67–81.

McCarn, Susan R., and Ruth E. Fassinger. "Revisioning Sexual Minority Identity Formation: A New Model of Lesbian Identity and Its Implications for Counseling and Research." *Counseling Psychologist* 24 (1996) 508–34.

Meyer, Ilan. "Prejudice, Social Stress, and Mental Health in Lesbian, Gay, and Bisexual Populations: Conceptual Issues and Research Evidence." *Psychological Bulletin* 129 (2003) 674–97.

Miles, Sara. *Take This Bread: A Radical Conversion.* New York: Ballentine Books, 2007.

Murr, Rachel. "'I Became Proud of Being Gay and Proud of Being Christian': The Faith Experiences of Queer Christian Women." *Journal of Religion & Spirituality in Social Work* 32 (2013) 349–72.

National Center for Transgender Equality. *Teaching Transgender.* Washington, DC: National Center for Transgender Equality, 2009. Online: http://transequality.org/Resources/NCTE_Teaching_Transgender.pdf.

Piper, John. "The Tornado, the Lutherans, and Homosexuality." *Desiring God* (blog), August 19, 2009. Online: http://www.desiringgod.org/blog/posts/the-tornado-the-lutherans-and-homosexuality.

Riggle, Ellen, Sharon Rostosky, Sharon Horne. "Marriage Amendments and Lesbian, Gay, and Bisexual Individuals in the 2006 Election," *Sexuality Research & Social Policy* 6 (2009) 80–89.

Rodriguez, Eric, and Suzanne Ouellette, "Gay and Lesbian Christians: Homosexual and Religious Identity Integration in the Members and Participants of a Gay-Positive Church." *Journal for the Scientific Study of Religion* 39 (2000) 39–53.

Rosario, Margaret, Ann Marie Yali, Joyce Hunter, and Marya Viorst Gwadz. "Religion and Health among Lesbian, Gay and Bisexual Youths: An Empirical Investigation and Theoretical Explanation." In *Sexual Orientation and Mental Health: Examining Identity and Development in Lesbian, Gay and Bisexual People*, by A. M. Omoto and H. S. Kurtzman, 117–40. Washington, DC: American Psychological Association, 2006.

Rostosky, Sharon Scales, Ellen D. B. Riggle, Sharon G. Horne, F. Nicholas Denton, and Julia Darnell Huellemeier. "Lesbian, Gay, and Bisexual Individuals' Psychological Reactions to Amendments Denying Access to Civil Marriage." *American Journal of Orthopsychiatry* 80 (2010) 302–10.

Ryan, Caitlin, David Huebner, Rafael Diaz, and Jorge Sanchez. "Family Rejection as a Predictor of Negative Health Outcomes in White and Latino Lesbian, Gay, and Bisexual Young Adults." *American Academy of Pediatrics* 123 (2013) 346–52.

Ryan, Caitlin, Stephen Russell, David Huebner, Rafael Diaz, and Jorge Sanchez. "Family Acceptance in Adolescence and the Health of LGBT Young Adults." *Journal of Child and Adolescent Psychiatric Nursing* 23 (2010) 205–13.

Savage, Dan, and Terry Miller, eds. *It Gets Better*. New York: Plume, 2012.

Savin-Williams, R. C. "Identity Development among Sexual-Minority Youth." In *Handbook of Identity Theory and Research*, ed. S. J. Schwartz, K. Luyckx, V. Vignoles, 671–89. New York: Springer, 2011.

Shapiro, Danielle, Desdamona Rios, and Abigail J. Stewart. "Conceptualizing Lesbian Sexual Identity Development: Narrative Accounts of Socializing Structures and Individual Decisions and Actions." *Feminism & Psychology* 20 (2010) 491–510.

Sherkat, D. E. "Sexuality and Religious Commitment in the United States: An Empirical Examination." *Journal for the Scientific Study of Religion* 41 (2002) 313–28.

Steffan, Melissa. "Alan Chambers Apologizes to Gay Community." *Christianity Today*, June 19, 2013. Online: http://www.christianitytoday.com/gleanings/2013/june/alan-chambers-apologizes-to-gay-community-exodus.html.

Wagner, G. "Integration of One's Religion and Homosexuality: A Weapon against Internalized Homophobia?" *Journal of Homosexuality* 26 (1994) 91–110.

Williams, Nancy R. "Spirituality and Religion in the Lives of Homeless Runaway Youth." *Journal of Religion & Spirituality in Social Work* 24 (2004) 47–66.